# THE TIMES
# BRITAIN
## FROM
# SPACE

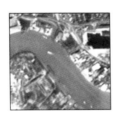

# THE TIMES
# BRITAIN
## FROM

# SPACE

TIMES BOOKS

First published in 2000 by
TIMES BOOKS
HarperCollins Publishers
77–85 Fulham Palace Road
London W6 8JB

The HarperCollins website address is
www.**fire**and**water**.com

British Library Cataloguing in Publication Data
A catalogue record for this book is available from
the British Library

ISBN 0 00 710584 3

**Colour origination by**
  Digital Imaging

**Printed and bound by**
  Bath Press, UK

All cartography derived from *The Times Comprehensive Atlas
of the World* 1999. Supplemented by *Collins Road Atlas of
Britain & Ireland.*

British Isles on pages 12-13

# Contents

**12**   British Isles

**14**   Cornwall
**16**   Devon
**18**   West Country (Bristol,
         Wiltshire, Somerset, Dorset)

**20**   Bristol
**22**   The Solent (Berkshire and
         Hampshire)
**24**   Isle of Wight (Portsmouth and
         The Solent)
**26**   Sussex (Brighton and
         the Downs)
**28**   Kent

**30**   Surrey
**32**   London (Greater London to
         the M25)
**34**   London (Central Boroughs)
**36**   Essex (The Stour, Blackwater
         and Crouch estuaries)
**38**   Cotswolds and Chilterns
         (Gloucstershire, Oxfordshire,
         Bedfordshire)

**40**   East Anglia (Norfolk, Suffolk,
         Cambridgeshire)
**42**   The Broads (Norwich, Great
         Yarmouth and Lowestoft)
**44**   The Fens (The Bedford Levels
         and the Isle of Ely)
**46**   Central England
**48**   West Midlands (Birmingham,
         Coventry and Wolverhampton)
**50**   Birmingham
**52**   Peak District
**54**   Lincolnshire (The Wash to
         The Humber)

# Britain from Space

Ever-changing, the landmass of Britain
makes an incredible and fascinating sight.
Its ragged outline, complete with
numerous inlets and peninsulas, tiny
islands and large promontories, provide
a distinct shape on any atlas page; a
kind of rogue piece from a jigsaw puzzle.

Looking down from the windows of an
aeroplane, the diversity becomes even
more apparent. Densely populated towns

and cities provide a stark contrast to the rolling hills, rivers and mountainous regions so often lying in close proximity.

Until now, aerial views from a plane have been the only means for most people to see this diverse and mesmerising landscape. Here, however, is an alternative view: **a view from space**. The stunning, high resolution photographs in this book were taken by satellite, and reveal the true landscape of modern day Britain. From the

dark, virtually untouched mass of Dartmoor, to the dense conurbation of major cities such as London, the limestone outcrops around Lancashire to the haunting mountains of Northern Scotland, these pictures collectively present a contemporary portrait of the country. Only from space is it possible to see how man and nature have worked to create this landscape; a view that includes Ice Age valleys, the Roman-built Hadrian's Wall, and modern structures such as the Humber Bridge.

## Satellite map technology

The images in this book were taken from an American civilian observation satellite, called Landsat 5. Launched by NASA in 1984, the satellite orbits the Earth at a height of 705.5 kilometres (438 miles) and at a speed of 27,000 kph (16,778 mph). It has seven sensors (blue/green/red/virtually infra-red/medium, infra-red and thermal infra-red), and moves around the planet in a relatively low orbit, which gives an extremely accurate view, called a 'scene'. To build up the map of a region or a whole country, several scenes have to be collated and then prepared during three key phases.

## Collation

Images are then collated digitally. As an example, the map of the British Isles has to be built up from 40 different scenes. There is an overlap area between two adjacent images of approximately 30 per cent, at a latitude of 45 degrees.

## Colour corrections

The rough images from Landsat 5 are bluish due to the thickness of the atmospheric layer. The natural colours are restored by re-mixing the intensity of the three colours (red, green and blue), which are the visible radiometries of the light spectrum. One of the major problems during this phase is to colour two neighbouring images uniformly as they are often obtained on different dates. This process makes seams invisible and ensures that only a single image is visible.

Not surprisingly, water appears as blue on the satellite pictures, while vegetation (forests, woodlands and grazing lands) is green, crops are usually yellow, bare earth is pale (almost white with yellow or brown shading) and snow is white. The variation in sea colours is due to differences in depth, marine currents and discharges from the estuaries, all helping to create a kaleidoscopic range of colours and tones.

## Geometrical corrections

Firstly, corrections are needed to make the shots accurate. This is because the spherical shape of the Earth, together with variations in satellite altitude, mean that the geometry of the rough scenes is deformed. Geometric corrections are therefore required so that each scene can be triangulated onto a known geographical location. This process also produces identification points for each scene and ensures that accurate maps, with grid references, are produced.

Approximately 60 points are identified for each scene before a specialist software package calculates the specific adjustments required. The necessary corrections are then made to the image, enabling the images to be collated without distortion of the 'seams'.

## Reading the images

The maps to the side of the images will help with the identification of landmarks. Major roads, waterways, motorways, railway lines, large ports such as Liverpool and Dover, airports including Heathrow and Gatwick, and large structures such as the Channel Tunnel, the two Severn Bridges and the Humber Bridge, are all apparent on both the map and the satellite image. Also visible are large natural landmarks, such as the sedimentary plains of London, the water catchment network of the British Isles (including the Severn, Thames and Trent) and large lakes, including the Scottish Lochs.

In addition to identifying specific places, however, it is also worth looking at the images in their entirety. Dense areas of habitation sit, perhaps incongruously, next to large, virtually untouched mountains, moors and national parks. Many of these land masses are now protected sites of national interest, but their unspoiled beauty is, historically, thanks to unfertile soil or an inhospitable environment. Similarly, meandering rivers can easily be identified as the focus for large, industrial areas, reflecting the historical significance of maritime waterways to the growth and development of the country. As such, these images of Britain serve also as a kind of historical portrait, revealing both its current appearance, and the geographical conditions that led to it.

# British Isles

The shape of the British Isles has been moulded over millions of years. The action of ice and water – both on the basic geology that has emerged from the earth's core, and that which has been deposited slowly out of ancient seas – has produced its current contours. Scotland is characterised by mountains which have been deeply scoured by ice. England has similar mountainous areas, but is mainly characterised by low lying areas constructed from solidified mud. The low lying areas are by far the most populated – the mountainous some of the most spectacular in Europe.

# Cornwall

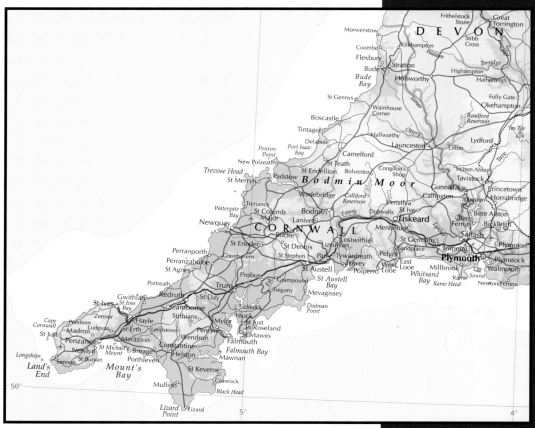

The tip of the southwest peninsula is characterised by two huge areas of granite – produced by upwellings of lava from the earth's interior that just failed to break through and produce volcanoes, instead they pushed up the land above them to produce Land's End and Bodmin Moor. The intense heat of the lava also caused dramatic changes to the surrounding rock, turning it into china clay. This is now extensively mined on the periphery of these areas, showing up as almost pure white scars on the landscape.

# Devon

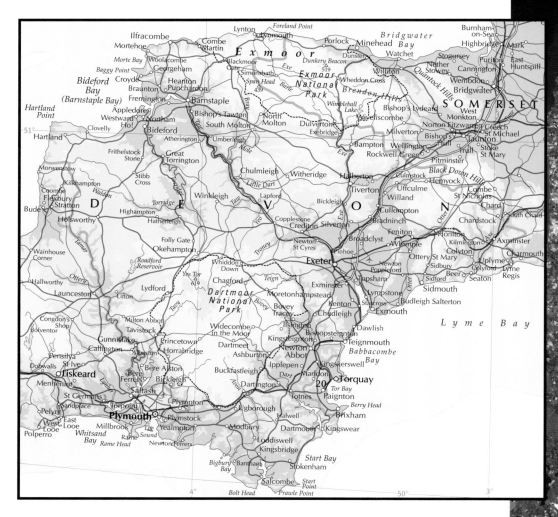

The huge bulk of Dartmoor dominates Devon, with its smaller partner Exmoor lying to the north. The country still retains the ancient field systems, so from the air it has one of the most complicated patterns of any county in England. On the south coast, Plymouth Sound and Salcombe Harbour are two of the best examples in Europe of rias or drowned river valleys. These were produced when the sea level rose by approximately 100–150 metres (328–492 feet) at the end of the last major Ice Age, subsequently drowning the river valleys that had been cut deep into the rock. In some places tree stumps remain in the floors of these rivers – remnants of the forests that grew on the banks 20,000 years ago.

# West Country

## (Bristol, Wiltshire, Somerset, Dorset)

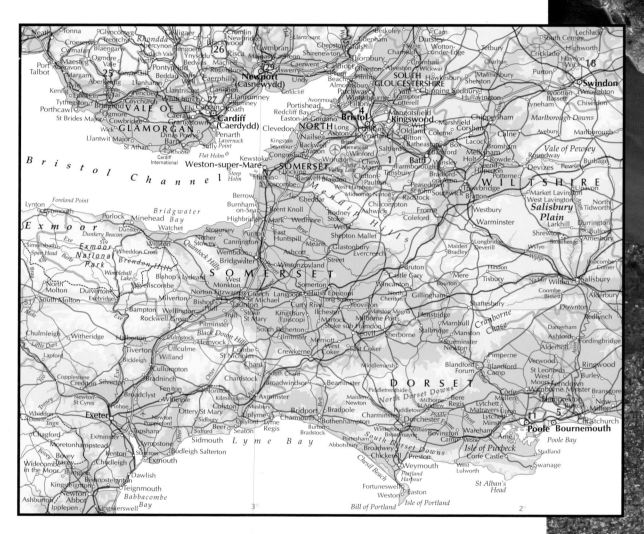

From above, the thin strip of land between the Severn Estuary and the English Channel looks much less substantial than the bulk of Devon to the west and Salisbury Plain to the east. As the Somerset Levels are entirely composed of reclaimed marshland – liable to be reclaimed by the sea at any instant and only defended from the English Channel by the chalk uplands, this strip seems even more precarious. Both sides are subjected to very strong tides – to the north the Bristol Channel scours England and Wales, with only the harder rocks of Steep Holm, Flat Holm and the Downs around Weston-super-Mare withstanding their inexorable work. On the south coast, the tides scour the face of Lyme Bay, depositing their work in the longest shingle beach in the UK – Chesil Beach.

# Bristol

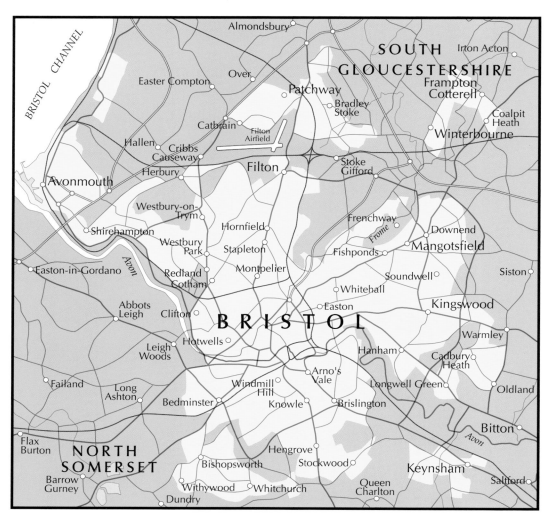

Bristol became one of Britain's major ports because it was the only safe, deep water port in the southern half of the island. This was because the port was hidden up the deep, fast flowing River Avon – far from the tidal treachery of the Severn Estuary. The River Avon had been an even more impressive river in earlier times – cutting a long, deep gorge through the limestone of the Bristol Downs in Clifton as the meltwater from the last great Ice Age rushed from the Salisbury Plains into the Severn Estuary. The gorge is now crossed by the Clifton Suspension Bridge – designed by Isambard Kingdom Brunel – for many years the longest suspension bridge in Britain. Brunel was also instrumental in the development of Bristol as a major railway hub for Wales and the southwest, as well as a shipbuilding centre.

In the 20th Century, Bristol became famous for its aircraft manufacturing – it is the home of the infamous Bristol Brabazon, one of the largest aircraft ever to fly and also the internationally famous aeroplane, Concorde. The works were based in the north of Bristol at Filton, site of the world's longest runway – now truncated by industrial development at its eastern end.

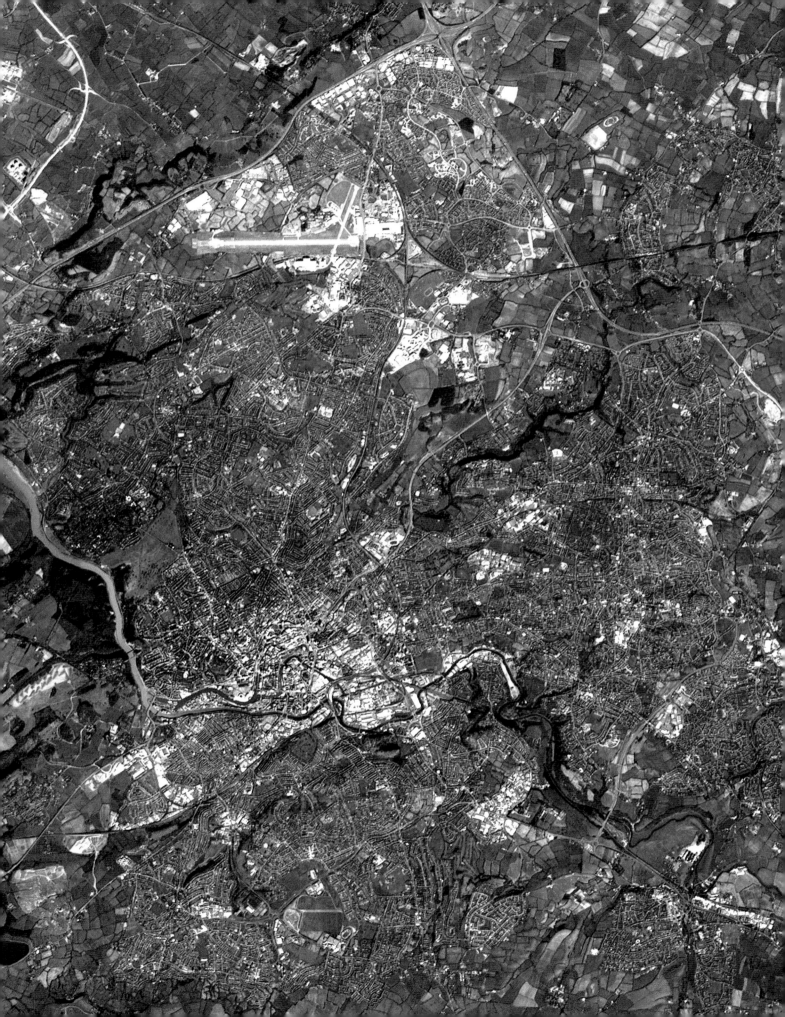

# The Solent

## (Berkshire and Hampshire)

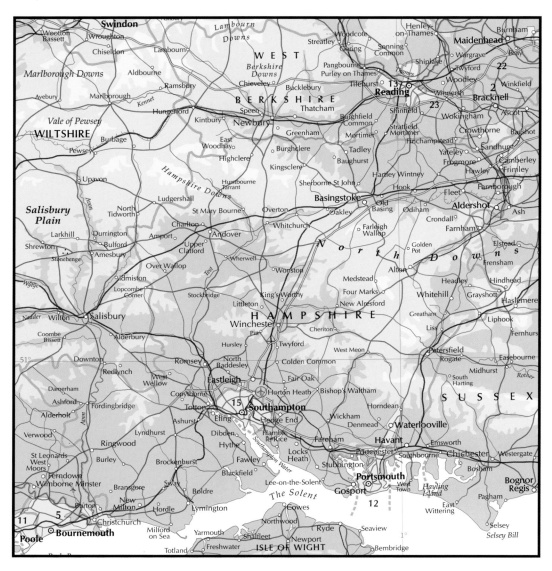

The chalk uplands of Salisbury Plain, South Downs and the Isle of Wight, surround the basin around Southampton in a complete ring. These uplands have been witness to one of the most extraordinary geological soap operas in the British Isles – the creation of The Solent and Isle of Wight. This drama began with a major river flowing from the highlands of Dartmoor East. The flow of this river cut though the chalk bowl of the Southampton basin in two points – the Needles in the west and the Bembridge Levels in the east – as the surrounding land was uplifted by the widening of the Atlantic and development of the Alps (which also caused the South Downs to be formed) – and then disappeared completely, leaving the rivers of the Isle of Purbeck and Isle of Wight flowing north as they have done for nearly 100 million years, when they should logically flow south.

# Isle of Wight

## (Portsmouth and The Solent)

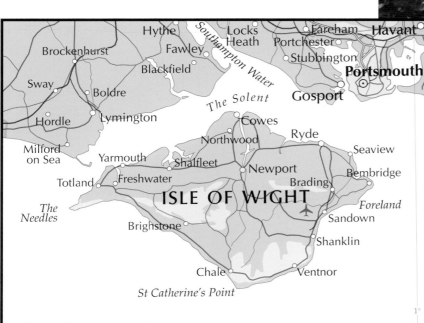

It is said that if the entire population of the world stood shoulder to shoulder, it would fit on the Isle of Wight – which perhaps goes to show what a large planet Earth really is. In the geological time scale its status as an island is only recent; it probably occurred around eight thousand years ago when sea levels rose after the last Ice Age, drowning an ancient river valley that now forms The Solent. The fact that "The Island", as it is fondly known by the locals, appears to have drifted away from the mainland and could be almost perfectly slotted back into it like a piece of a jigsaw, is nothing more than coincidence. The landscape continues to change, the crumbling clay and sandstone cliffs of the southwest coast being particularly vulnerable to marine erosion. This area, notably around Chale, has also earned a reputation as Britain's dinosaur capital, cliff falls regularly revealing the remains of previous "residents" who ruled this part of the world over one hundred million years ago. Then, the Isle of Wight was part of an enormous swamp and lagoon on a latitude similar to present-day Cairo. Today, tourism is the principal industry, with visitors enjoying unique features such as the chalk stacks of The Needles, Alum Bay's coloured sands, (of which there are officially twenty-one shades), and the abundance of public footpaths – of which there are more miles than public road.

# Sussex

## (Brighton and the Downs)

The enormous expanse of chalk that makes up the Downs is nothing less than the stuff of life. Epochs ago the entire region lay beneath the sea; when the tiny creatures whose home this was died, their bodies sank to the sea bed, their shells

and skeletons accumulating over millions of years to create a thick layer of chalk. The subsequent formation of the Alps caused the chalk to uplift into a massive dome, since breached by the English Channel. Elsewhere, the forces of erosion have left just two principal chalk fingers – one of which forms the South Downs. The initial impression of the Downs is one of gentle, rolling countryside, but it is at the coast that the scenery is at its most spectacular. Nowhere is this more apparent than east of Seaford at the Seven Sisters cliffs, (there are really eight), and the towering headland at Beachy Head, 183 metres (600 feet) above sea level. (Beachy is derived from the French beau chef – "beautiful headland"). Inland, the chalk dome has been eroded to reveal the clays and sandstones that form the High Weald Area of Outstanding Natural Beauty, epitomised by Ashdown Forest, once a royal hunting ground, and inspiration for the world famous *Winnie the Pooh* stories.

# Kent

The North Downs are the second great finger of chalk, which was once the dome that formed the land bridge to France. To their west lie the alluvial deposits that are the flat, bleak landscape of Romney Marsh, much of which has been reclaimed by man from the sea – a great deal still lies at or near sea level. While much of the Marsh remains extremely vulnerable to marine forces, the shingle spit of Dungeness has, conversely, been successively built up by centuries of longshore drift. Its old shorelines are plainly visible and it is still growing. Unlike their South Down cousins, the North Downs lie principally inland, starting in northern Surrey and culminating in the world-famous White Cliffs of Dover. Their tradition of being variously the first and last landfall of arriving and departing cross-Channel travellers has been diminished somewhat by the construction of the Channel Tunnel, whose terminal shows up here as a large white gash, just inland of Folkestone. The Isle of Thanet is no longer an island, although at the time the Romans arrived it was separated from the mainland by a channel that ran roughly between Herne Bay and Sandwich.

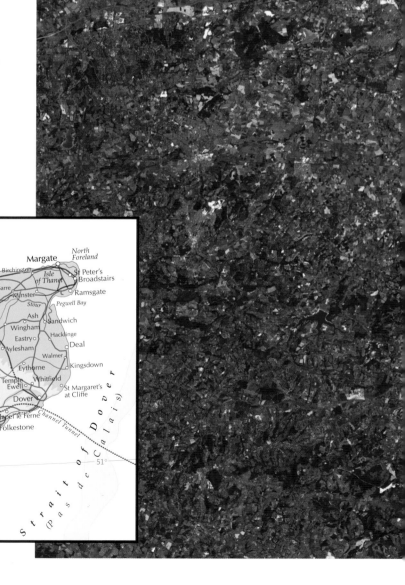

# Surrey

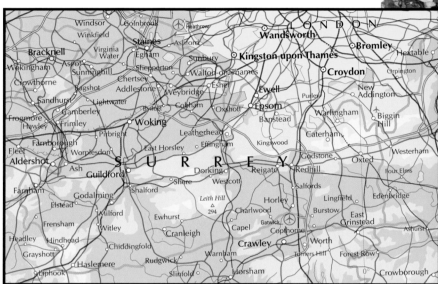

It is in the vicinity of Guildford, the county town of Surrey, that the North Downs start their march to the sea. They reach their pinnacle at Leith Hill which, at a height of 291 metres (955 feet), is the highest point in South-East England. With its breath-taking views it is said that on an extremely clear day you can see the English Channel from here. The remainder of the county is comprised mainly of clays and sandstones, much of which is heathland, but none the less spectacular. The Devil's Punchbowl, near Hindhead, is particularly note-worthy, appearing as though a giant has scooped a large handful out of the landscape. It is this combination of countryside and easy access to London that has led to much of the county falling into the Stockbroker Belt; with an average of six residents per hectare, Surrey is one of the most densely populated non-metropolitan counties in England. The M25, known to many as "the World's largest car park", snakes across the landscape while Gatwick, London's second airport and formerly in Surrey, became part of West Sussex as a result of the 1974 local boundary changes.

# London

## (Greater London to the M25)

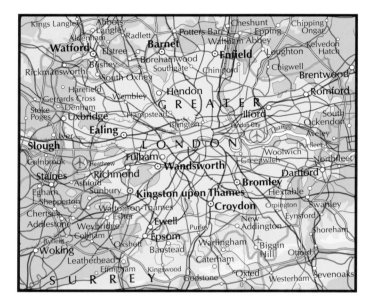

Around seven million people live in the thirty-two boroughs of Greater London. Arguably its name is something of a misnomer, for not only does Greater London include all the outlying boroughs but also, somewhat confusingly, the central areas such as the City Of Westminster and the City of London. In recent years Greater London has been colloquially taken to mean the entire area contained within the M25, London's orbital motorway; demographically and geographically this is far from accurate – though precisely where "London" begins is anybody's guess.

For hundreds of years, London Bridge was the lowest point downstream at which the Thames was bridged, a status subsequently acquired by Tower Bridge in 1894 and more recently by the new Queen Elizabeth II Bridge at Dartford, which effectively doubled the capacity of the congested Dartford Tunnel. The bridge is clearly seen on the far right. Heathrow, meanwhile, continues to mushroom as the world's busiest international airport, with plans afoot for still further development. The water features to its south are mostly reservoirs, with the occasional gravel pit.

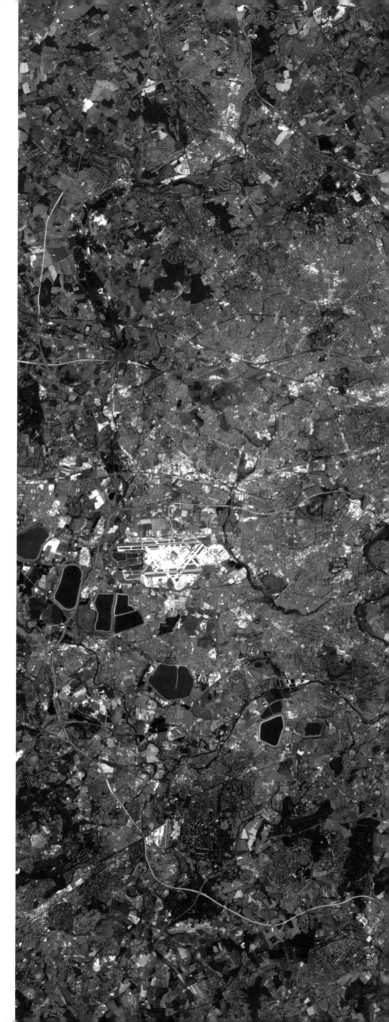

# London

## (Central Boroughs)

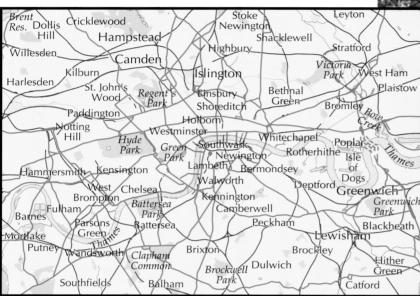

The twelve central London boroughs, (including Westminster, but not The City), are home to almost two and a half million people – around 4 per cent of the UK's population. For all that, some notable areas of "green" remain, not least Hyde Park, Regent's Park and Greenwich Park – through which the Meridian Line, zero degrees longitude, passes. When the Romans arrived in Britain during the 1st Century, they built Londinium on two small hills just North of where now stands London Bridge – not least since most of the surrounding terrain comprised marshland. To this day it remains a fact that much of central London is built largely on a sinking geological basin which, as it continues to subside, is a cause for ever-increasing concern. For centuries, the Thames was the capital's lifeline to trading with the outside world and, as the vessels that used it became ever larger, it became necessary to build special docks, typified by those on the Isle of Dogs. These are now used for recreational purposes and are the sites of some of the capital's most exclusive, and expensive, residential developments.

# Essex

## (The Stour, Blackwater and Crouch estuaries)

Essex was one of the seven original Anglo-Saxon kingdoms, its name originating from the Old English "East-Seaxe". Perhaps a little confusingly, however, Mersea Island in the Blackwater estuary is entirely unrelated to the similar-sounding Saxon kingdom of Mercia: this was in central England. Mimicking nearby East Anglia, of which most of Essex is not strictly part, the topography is largely flat. The coastline is characterised by several estuaries, notably those of the Thames, Blackwater and Crouch. Of these the presence of man is most felt along the Thames estuary, particularly at Canvey Island, (whose insular status is only barely maintained by a narrow creek), where oil

refineries predominate. It hit the headlines in 1953 when floods caused by onshore gales and unusually high tides claimed fifty-eight lives. The resort of Southend-on-Sea, at the estuary's easternmost extremity and long the playground of Londoners, gained fame for having the world's longest pier. In the northeast of the county, Colchester proudly lays claim to being the oldest town in Britain: to the Romans it was Camulodunum, but even before their arrival it was probably the capital of a kingdom belonging to Cunobelin – better known in his guise of Shakespeare's Cymbeline. On a more recent note, London's third airport, Stansted, shows up as a white rectangle to the far left.

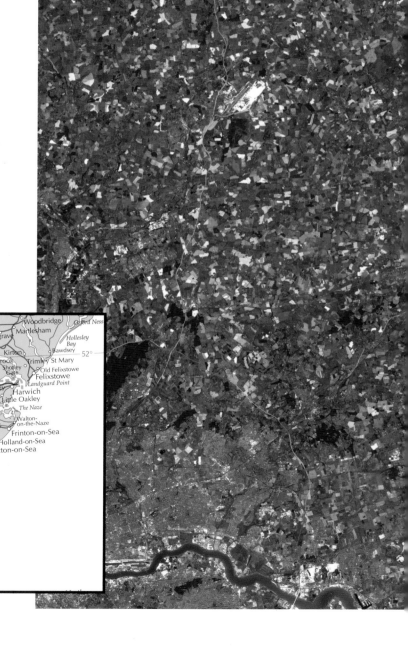

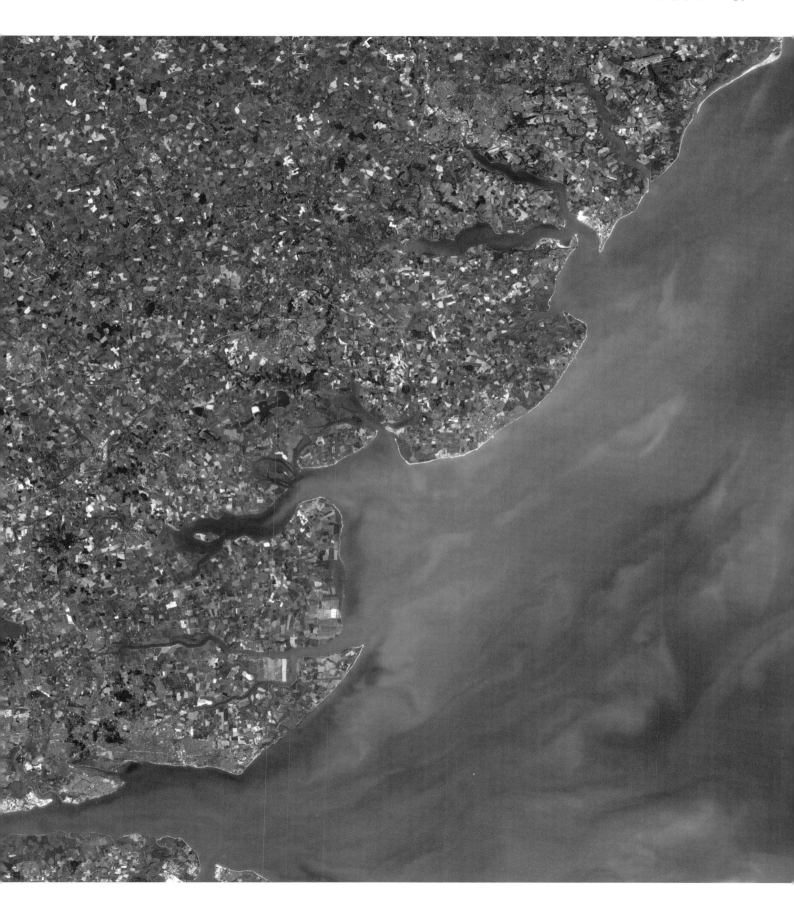

# Cotswolds and Chilterns

(Gloucestershire, Oxfordshire, Buckinghamshire, Bedfordshire)

The limestone and chalk that respectively form the Cotswolds and Chilterns give rise to a landscape that is home to towns and villages of chocolate box beauty. The area encompassed to the southeast of the Chilterns has become extremely popular with London commuters, a process started by the expansion northwest of the Metropolitan Railway and the development of "Metroland". Parts of the Cotswolds rise to over 305 metres (1000 feet) above sea level – Cleeve Hill, just east of Broadway being a particularly spectacular viewpoint – but such heights are the exception rather than the rule. The limestone, or "Cotswold stone" as it is better known, features widely as an extremely attractive building material which is at its best under the low light of sunrise or sunset. The villages of Bourton-on-the-Water and Stow-on-the-Wold are built almost entirely of the stone, and probably have their origins way back in the 12th or 13th Centuries, stonemasonry even then being a well-established skill. Nor is it just the villages that catch the eye: Oxford is a city of jaw-droppingly stunning beauty. It owes its existence to the fact that it was a convenient crossing point of the River Thames, that here temporarily becomes the Isis. Literally it was "the ford where oxen cross". Its academic reputation probably originated in the 12th Century, although nobody is certain.

# East Anglia

(Norfolk, Suffolk, Cambridgeshire)

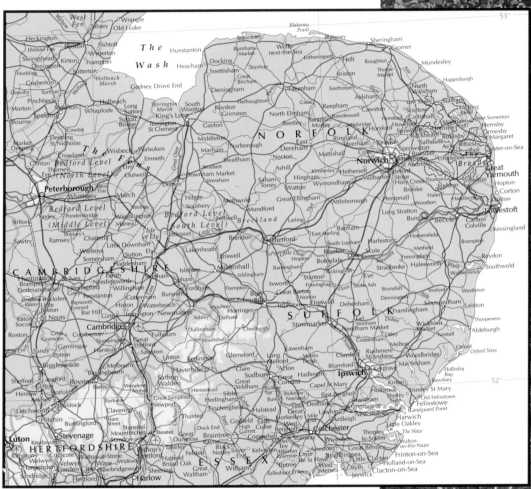

East Anglia is characterised by flat lowlands that seldom exceed 91 metres (300 feet) above sea level. Geologically, its "natural" rock is split fifty-fifty between chalk in the west and clay in the east. The area also marked the southernmost advance of the vast ice sheets that covered most of Britain during the last Ice Age; this has resulted in the natural bedrock being covered by glacial deposits of boulder clay and gravels that are, in places, well over 30.5 metres (100 feet) deep. These, together with the peaty soil of the drained Fenlands and alluvial river deposits, have made the area ideal for agriculture, reflected by the fact that around 25 per cent of Britain's vegetables are grown here. There is also a strong tradition of sea-faring; in times past, the region's proximity to the Continent made it an important trading centre, particularly in wool.

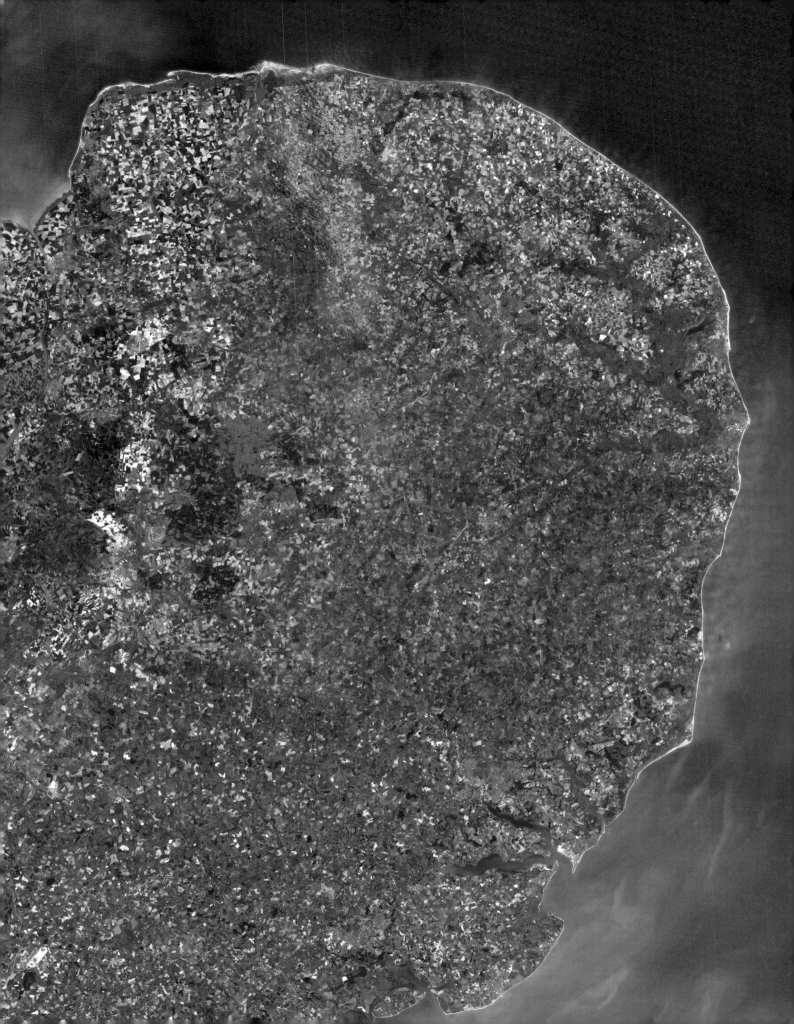

# The Broads

## (Norwich, Great Yarmouth and Lowestoft)

The Norfolk Broads were long a puzzle to geologists who, for many years, considered them to be flooded river valleys. However, they are not a natural phenomena at all, rather flooded ancient peat workings. Even so, prior to the extraction of peat the area was almost certainly estuarial on a massive scale. Shallow in nature, the Broads are linked by a series of rivers that slowly make their way across the flat landscape towards the coast. There are around forty Broads of varying sizes, of which Breydon Water is one of the largest. It is into this that the area's three principal rivers coincidentally drain before reaching the sea at nearby

Great Yarmouth, an ancient fishing port and setting for part of Charles Dickens's *David Copperfield*. In all, the Broads and their associated rivers offer almost 209km (130 miles) of navigable waterway, so it is little surprise that boating is a popular pastime and major source of employment. Other than on the coastal strip, settlements have tended to develop on higher ground not subject to flooding, to which the region was long susceptible. Until two hundred years ago Norwich, the regional capital, ranked second only to London in importance – a reflection of its status gained largely through the export of textiles and wool.

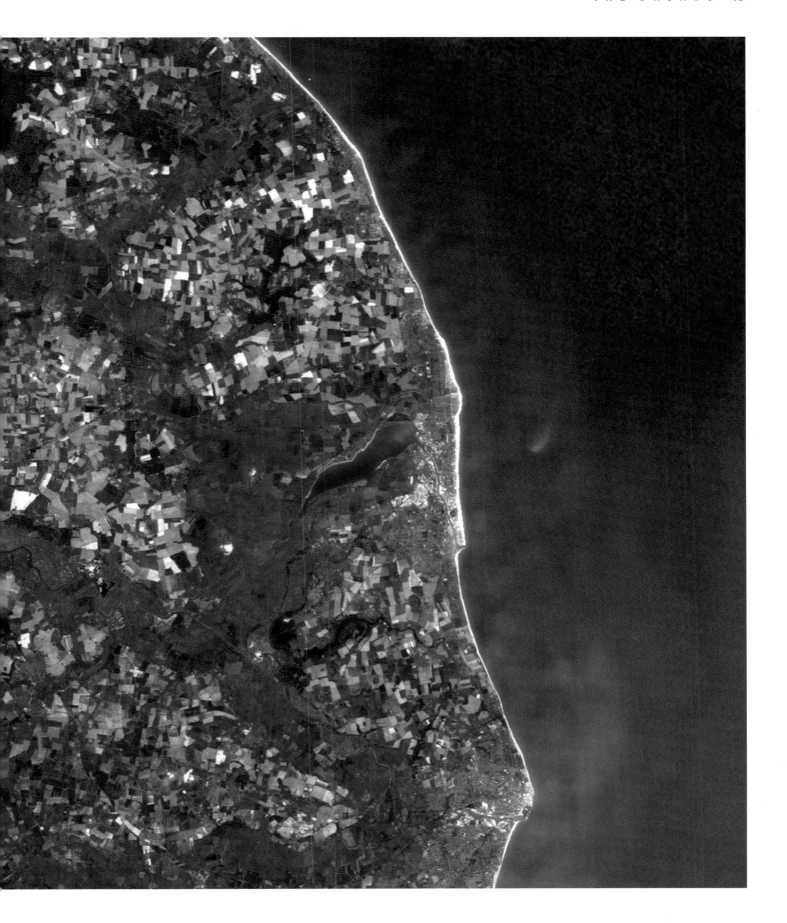

# The Fens

## (The Bedford Levels and the Isle of Ely)

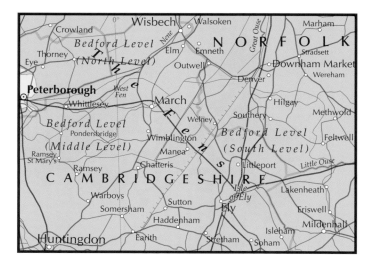

Although the underlying rock is primarily clay, the vast majority of Fenland is comprised of silts, gravels and peat. These contribute towards making it one of the most fertile regions in Britain, although in its natural state the area was little more than swamp and marsh. Drainage and reclamation by man started in the 17th Century, subsequently ensuring that little natural fenland now remains. The predominantly marshy nature of the landscape restricted settlement to islets of gravel or boulder clay, the classic example being the city of Ely, which originally was literally island-bound. (Many consider that its name is the Ancient Briton for "Eel Island".) Accordingly, its magnificent cathedral, dating from the 11th Century, acts as a beacon for miles around. What appears to be a large slash running diagonally across the landscape is actually formed by the parallel New Bedford Cut and Old Bedford Cut, two principal drainage channels. They are named after the 17th Century Duke of Bedford who first instigated the wholesale drainage of the area.

# Central England

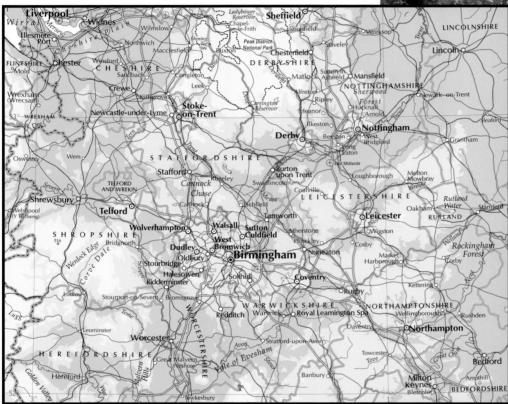

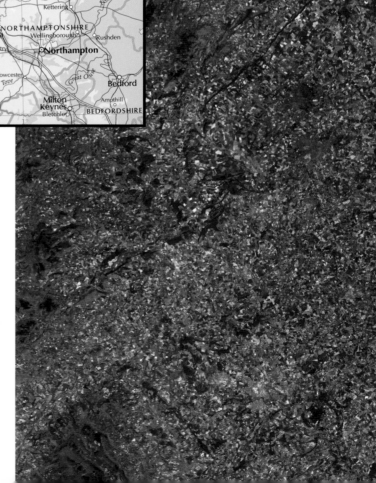

On a journey north through Britain, it is in Central England that the first hints of a predominantly industrial landscape come to light. It is a reputation held longer by some places than others. Birmingham, for example, was of little significance until the advent of the later stages of the Industrial Revolution; Northampton, (shoes), Stoke on Trent, (pottery), and Sheffield, (steel), have far longer manufacturing pedigrees, often in excess of five hundred years. So it is easy to overlook the fact that the region possesses some of Britain's most varying scenery. The Vale of Evesham, the fine limestone escarpment of Wenlock Edge, the granite ridge of the Malvern Hills, and the limestone peaks of the Peak District National Park handsomely demonstrate the point. Not all features, however, are of Mother Nature's making: Rutland, England's smallest county, is home to Britain's largest man-made lake, Rutland Water. Covering over 3,000 acres, it supplies water to much of the East Midlands.

# West Midlands

(Birmingham, Coventry and Wolverhampton)

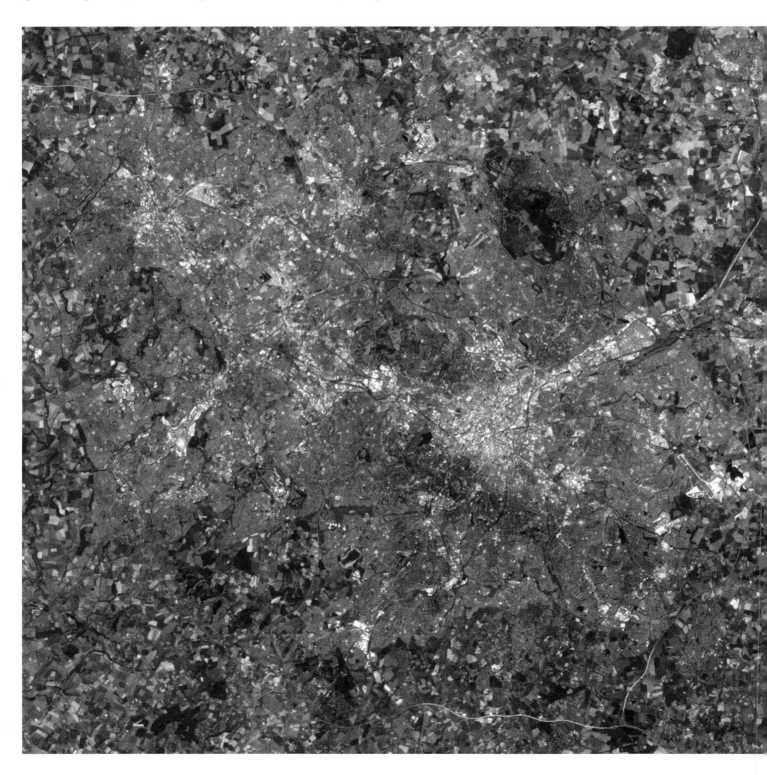

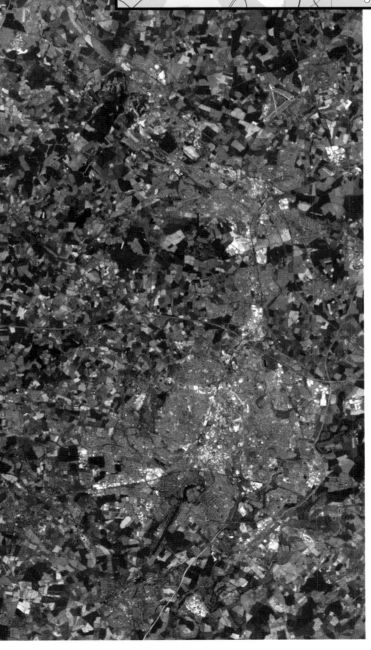

Looking from space, it almost seems as though somebody has flicked a gigantic brush, liberally loaded with white paint, across the landscape. Without doubt, the towns and cities that make up the West Midlands conurbation dominate this picture. Falling into the category of a Metropolitan Council, the conurbation came into being in 1974 following the 1972 Local Government Act. It is made up of seven districts: Oldbury, Solihull, Dudley, Wolverhampton, Birmingham, Walsall and Coventry – all of which formerly fell within the purview of the respective counties in which they were located. (Birmingham, for example, was part of Warwickshire). Covering an area of approximately 906 square kilometres (350 square miles), it is home to over two and half million people. Whilst it is now one of the most densely populated areas of Britain, prior to the Industrial Revolution there were very few settlements at all. Now it is difficult to see where one town ends, and the next begins. The predominance of canals, among them the Staffordshire & Worcestershire, the Birmingham Main, and the Wyrley & Essington Canals – all of them in the vicinity of West Bromwich – serve as testimony that the region has played an important role in the industrial development of the nation.

# Birmingham

The story of England's second largest city is one of growth on an unprecedented scale protracted over many years. Nevertheless, even at the height of the Industrial Revolution fewer than 250,000 people lived here: now Birmingham, or Brum as its residents like to call it, is home to over a million. The industrial areas of today's city show up clearly, as do the tightly packed residential suburbs that predominate to the south. Its success as an industrial centre is due in no small part to the fact that it is virtually in the "middle" of England, an attribute recognised by the early industrialists who built a fine network of canals and, later, railways to exploit its enviable location. To a degree the tradition has continued in recent years with the building of motorways and roads that climax at Gravelly Hill in the wonderful concrete knot that is Spaghetti Junction. Although it is often argued that poor 20th Century town planning has done little to enhance it, Birmingham nevertheless has its fair share of culture and, yes, beauty – the 18th Century splendour of St.Philip's Cathedral for example. Meanwhile, the Botanical Gardens will be found in the mainly residential suburb of Edgbaston. They are, perhaps, the jewel in the crown of Birmingham's one hundred plus parks. Much of the city and its environs are said to have inspired the author J R R Tolkein who, as a youth, lived here for many years.

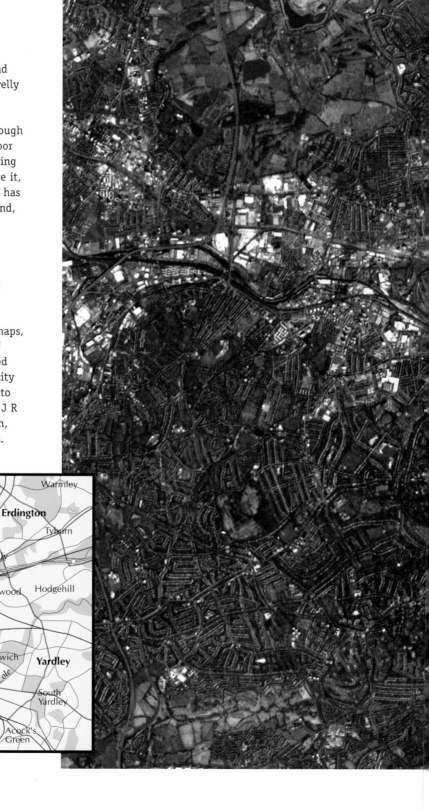

# Peak District

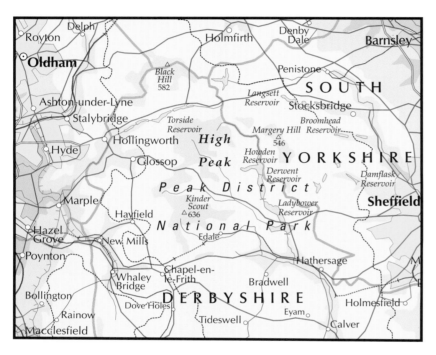

The first impression gained by many visitors to the Peak District is that of a landscape dominated by limestone. This is not strictly accurate, for while it does indeed predominate in many areas, there are extensive deposits of shales and millstone grit. High Peak is a splendid example of the latter and it is here, at Kinder Scout, that the highest point of the district can be found – 636 metres (2087 feet) above sea level. (How strange it seems that one of England's highest points once lay beneath a shallow sea.) The area revels in the accolade of being awarded two "firsts": following a 1949 Act of Parliament, the Peak District became Britain's first National Park, (over 1424 square kilometres/550 square miles now fall within its boundaries); and in 1965, the Pennine Way, which crosses the North West corner of the Park, became Britain's first long-distance footpath. Hardly surprisingly, the area attracts a huge number of visitors anxious to enjoy the varied range of leisure facilities it offers. These include long-distance walking, rock climbing and pot holing in the numerous limestone caverns. The Ladybower and Derwent reservoirs, clearly seen, are man-made and were completed in 1939 by flooding two natural river valleys. The Derwent reservoir was used in 1943 for dummy runs by the famous Dambusters.

# Lincolnshire

## (The Wash to The Humber)

In all likelihood The Wash was dammed by one of the southernmost glaciers of the last Ice Age, causing the rivers that flow into it to create a vast lake far inland of the present coastline and the Humber Estuary. The sites of present-day Wisbech and Boston would almost certainly have been under water, although Lincoln would not by virtue of the fact that it lay on a slightly higher ridge. Further north, Grimsby would have lain beneath the ice. In thousands of years hence, The Wash will probably disappear altogether, silted up by the rivers that discharge into it. The landscape is generally flat and low-lying in nature, the principal exception being the Lincolnshire Wolds. Covering around 5845.5 square kilometres (2,250 square miles), much of the county is under agricultural use, with Spalding and its environs gaining a reputation for the cultivation of bulbs. Even so, Lincolnshire is home to over 600,000 people, over 80,000 of whom live in Lincoln, the county town. It was founded by the Romans who were doubtless attracted by the fact that it lay on a hill top. It, and the other principal towns of Grimsby and Boston show up splendidly here.

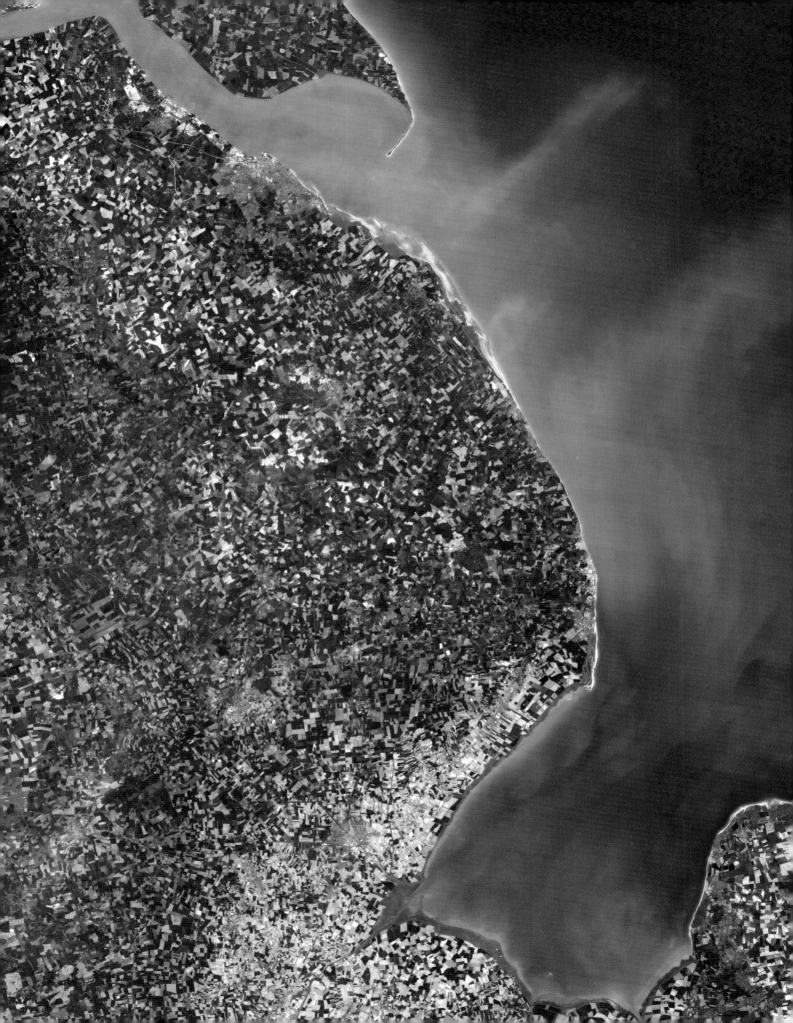

# Yorkshire

## (North, West and East Ridings)

What was once England's largest county has subsequently been split by the 1972 Local Government Act, and a succession of subsequent changes, into a series of smaller counties and unitary authorities. Prior to this, it was administratively divided into the North, East and West Ridings, terms that are still in common use today. (The term "Riding" is of Anglo-Saxon origin, and derives from "thriding" – literally translated as "one third"). The topography varies enormously: limestone and millstone grit – an extremely hard rock which was put to good use well before the advent of the Industrial Revolution – are the principal constituents of the Pennines in the west of the region. They are often referred to as the "backbone of England", as well as mountains – which they certainly are not. Conversely, the North York Moors mainly comprise of far softer sandstone. They were designated a National Park in 1952, to be followed two years later by the Yorkshire Dales. On the eastern coastal fringe chalk briefly appears, notably at Flamborough Head.

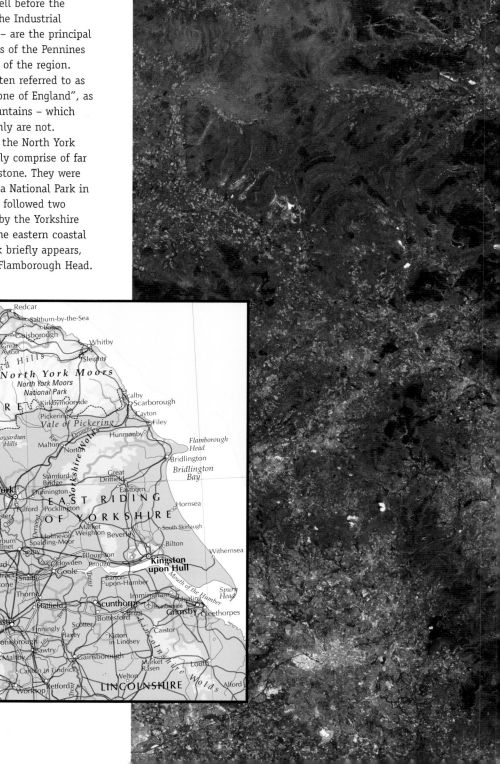

# West Yorks
## (Leeds and Bradford)

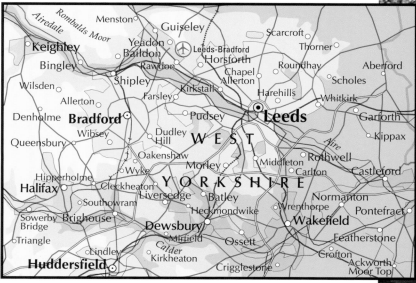

It was plentiful supplies of coal and water that brought manufacturing industry here in a big way. Leeds, Wakefield, Huddersfield, Bradford and Dewsbury all built their prosperity on one variant or other of the long-established textile industry. While the Industrial Revolution changed the face of textile manufacture for good, it is also often associated with an intolerable working environment and living conditions of great squalor. This was not entirely the case, however: a leading light in social reform, the industrialist Titus Oates built Saltaire, an entire new village just north of Bradford to house his cloth mills; he also provided living accommodation for his

workers. Industry is now more diverse, with textiles being less important; indeed, the area has become an important regional business centre with its own airport, (Leeds Bradford), at Yeadon. Against all expectations, both Leeds and Bradford are important cultural and heritage centres: Leeds has some superb architecture, (*viz*. the Town Hall), and museums – particularly in the Royal Armouries. Not to be outdone, Bradford has its cathedral, marvellously Gothic City Hall and the splendid National Museum of Photography, Film and Television. The River Aire, meanwhile, upon which much of the region's prosperity was founded, slinks unconcerned just North of both cities.

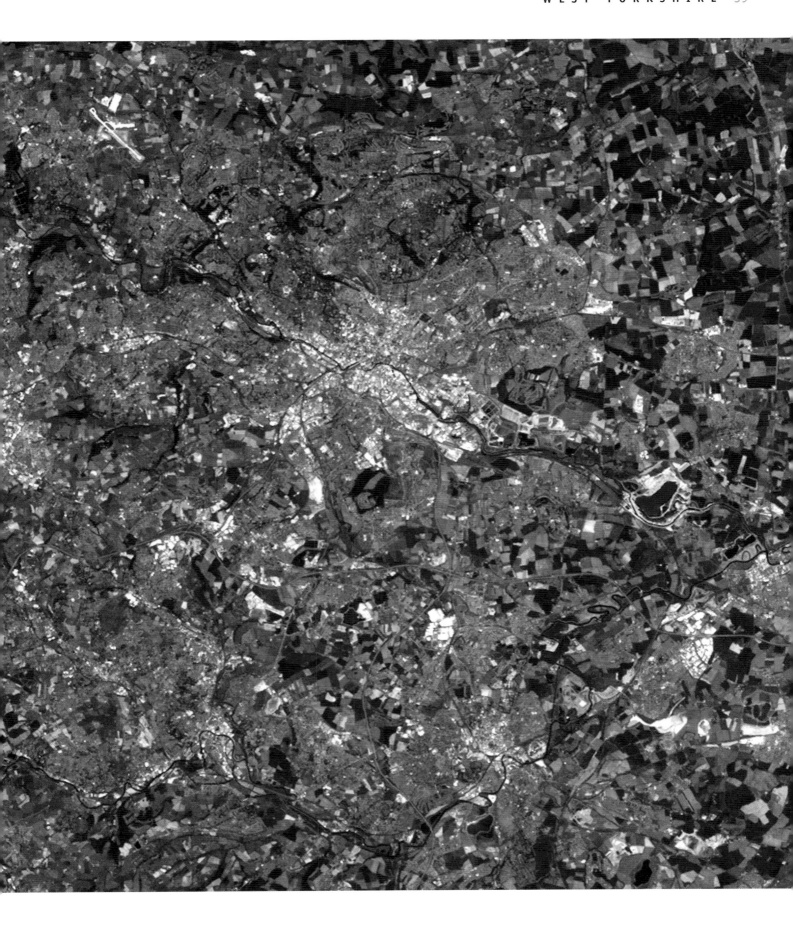

# Sheffield

## (Rotherham and Doncaster)

Looking from space like a rotating Catherine Wheel, the industrial city of Sheffield was founded on the River Don – which shows up particularly well on the top right of this photograph. There can hardly be a household in the country that at one time did not own something made here: naturally, think of Sheffield, think of steel, think of cutlery. However, in the bigger picture, steel is but a recent innovation; the city's fortune and fame was founded on iron, and with this particular commodity Sheffield has been linked for nigh on one thousands years. In the great days of heavy steel manufacture, the Don appeared to be almost one continuous steelworks from Sheffield to Rotherham, but cheap foreign imports now mean that more specialised forms of the industry are just as important. These include the manufacture of alloys, electro-plating and, of course, the ever-famous cutlery. Particularly notable from this picture is the predominance of lakes to the west of the city; they are, in fact, almost exclusively reservoirs. Sheffield is home to half a million people, Rotherham, (of Roman origin), 250,000 and Doncaster, (Danum to the Romans), 290,000.

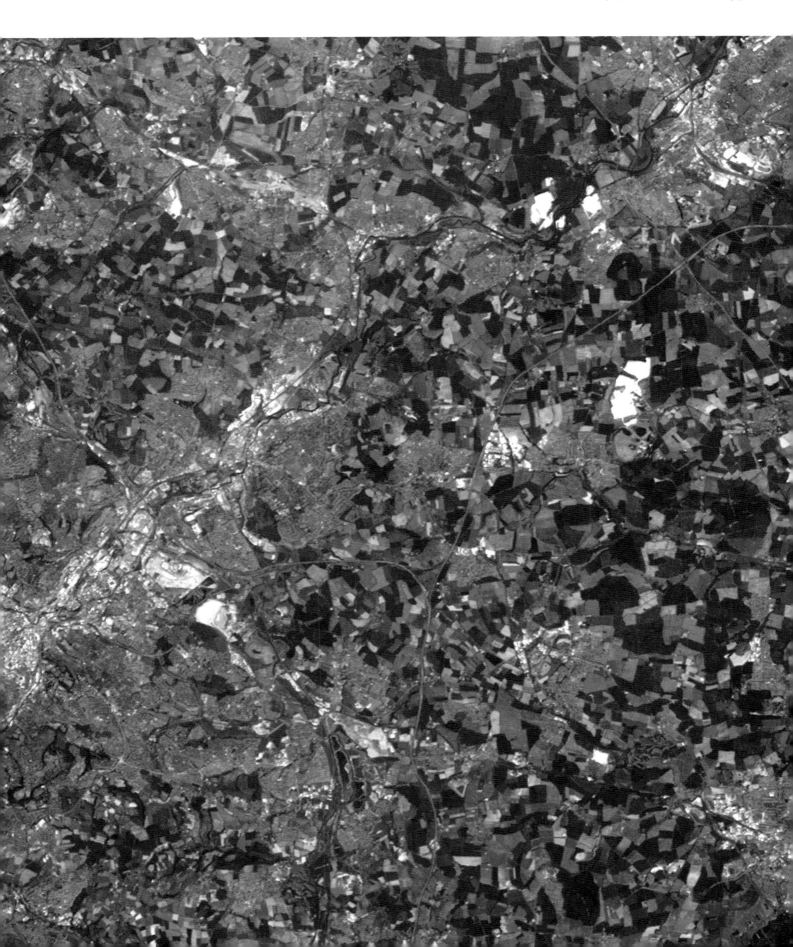

# Yorkshire Moors

At just over 1424 square kilometres (550 square miles), Britain's fifth largest National Park dominates the landscape; the marked cessation of agricultural land where moorland takes over is all too plain to see, especially to the west. The topography of the region is also reflected in its drainage pattern; with only rare exceptions, the majority of rivers drain north/south, ultimately finding their way into the Derwent. The occasional forests that appear to spring out of nowhere are largely planted by man. With an absolute dearth of roads, and indeed human habitation, the area, (in some places over 305 metres/1000 feet above sea level), can at times seem to be exceedingly bleak. But it is also a place of stark beauty, which is why it has gained such popularity with walkers. The harsh terrain means that the few pockets of population are generally restricted to the coast, notably at Scarborough, (population around 55,000), whose headland location shows up like a small bump. Long a lively and celebrated holiday resort, it was originally a spa town – subsequently finding fame as a favourite spot for the growing Victorian trend of sea bathing. Further north, the pretty seaside town of Whitby is also a popular centre for visitors, many of whom are drawn by its links with Count Dracula – who surely would have felt quite at home in the bleakness of the nearby moors.

Middlesbrough
Skelton
Saltburn-by-the-Sea
Brotton
Stockton-on-Tees
REDCAR AND
Loftus
Hinderwell
Guisborough
CLEVELAND
Thornaby-on-Tees
Roseberry Topping
Sandsend
Whitby
Yarm
320
High Hawsker
Kirklevington
Great
Danby
Stokesley
Ayton
Egton
Sleights
Castleton
Robin Hood's Bay
Hutton
Great Broughton
Grosmont
Rudby
Cleveland Hills
Goathland
Cod Beck
Round
North York Moors
Staintondale
Brompton
Hill
Rosedale Abbey
Cloughton
nby
454
Hackness
Burniston
Hambleton Hills
North York Moors
Hawnby
Gillamoor
National Park
Lockton
Scalby
Scarborough
Knayton
Rye
Dove
Wrelton
Boltby
Kirkbymoorside
Eastfield
Cayton
Thirsk
YORKSHIRE
Helmsley
Pickering
Thornton Dale
Seamer
Filey
Sproxton
Riccal
Vale of Pickering
Staxton
Sowerby
Wass
Severn
Snainton
Coxwold
Oswaldkirk
1
Derwent
West Knapton
Hunmanby

# The Humber

## (Kingston upon Hull and Grimsby)

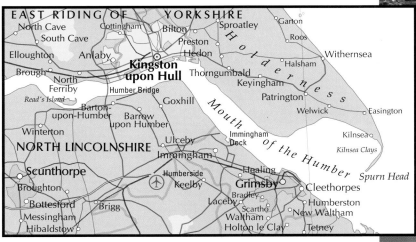

During the last Ice Age almost the entire Humber Estuary lay beneath a great glacier; only its western-most extremity escaped the ice's frosty advance. Thus the landscape we now see was, at least in geological terms, created only yesterday. There are two particularly striking features on this photograph: the first, Spurn Point, is one of Britain's finest examples of a spit. In places only a few feet above sea level, it clings tenaciously, hook-like, to the mainland. Its very existence is only at the expense of land elsewhere, being primarily composed of material that has been eroded from the coast further north and subsequently deposited here. Indeed, the story of Holderness in general, of

which the spit forms the southernmost part, is much the same – albeit on a far larger scale. It probably started life as a small island formed of eroded material carried south by the sea. The second notable feature, conversely, is man-made: the Humber Bridge was opened in 1981, and with a span of over 1402 metres (4,600 feet) it was, at the time, the longest bridge in the world. Importantly, it cut many miles from the journey between the towns of north and south Humberside. Kingston-upon-Hull, coloquially known simply as Hull, is the region's principal town with a history dating back to at least the 13th Century. Then, as now, it had a great tradition of sea-faring.

# Lancashire

First thoughts of Lancashire are of a densely populated, heavily industrialised county founded on the manufacture of textiles and cotton – which, to a certain extent, is true. However, were Merseyside and Greater Manchester to be excluded, (as indeed they should, being "independent" metropolitan counties), then Lancashire appears in an entirely different light. Either way, it is the oft-overlooked north that is of a more rural nature, with spectacular scenery to match. In common with many English "forests", the Forest of Bowland is hardly forest in the modern perceived sense of the word; heath and moorland is probably more accurate, the term forest being traditionally used in its ancient legal sense of being the monarch's hunting ground. The landscape is predominantly based on limestone and millstone grit, although there are local deposits of shale, whose base "ingredient" is compressed clay. On the coast the limestone is at its most impressive on Morecambe Bay's craggy outcrops, particularly in the vicinity of Warton. The bay is also home to one of Britain's largest areas of mudflat, continuously growing and with an enormous tidal range. Further south, the Ribble estuary is the site of one of Britain's largest nature reserves, while the attributes of nearby Blackpool are well-known.

# Manchester

## (Stockport and Oldham)

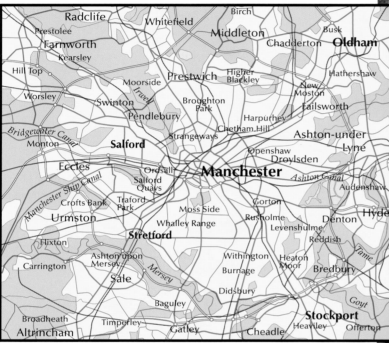

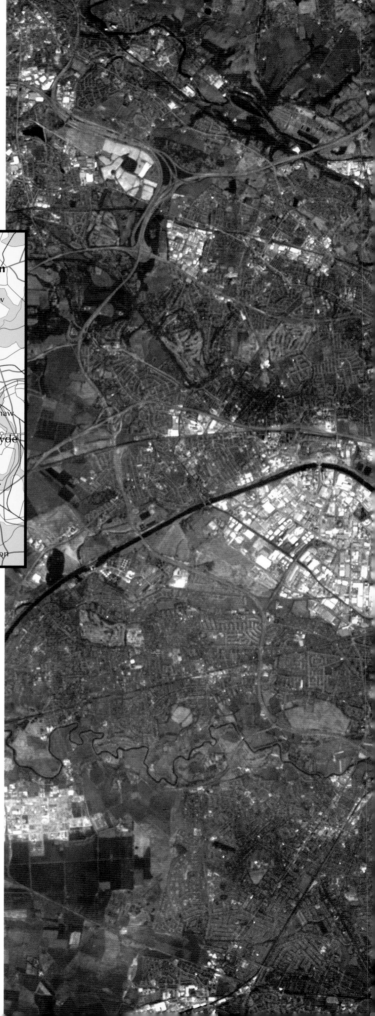

The city of Manchester is home to over 400,000 people – around one fifth of the Greater Manchester area that includes Bolton, Oldham, Rochdale, Salford, Stockport and Wigan. Traditionally associated with the 18th Century cotton industry, (cotton production, if not exactly an "industry", probably started a couple of hundred years earlier), its history is far longer. To the Romans it was Mancunium; their legacy lives on by virtue of the fact that Manchester's natives are still known as Mancunians. The Saxons built their settlement on almost exactly the same spot, (close to where the cathedral now stands). Above all, it is probably the city's role in the development of transport and communications that led to its industrial prosperity. The Bridgewater Canal, completed in 1761 and linking the Duke of Bridgewater's coal mines with the city, was Britain's first true canal. Numerous other canals followed, and trade was boosted further with the opening, in 1894, of the 56km (35 mile) long Manchester Ship Canal, linking Manchester's Salford Quays with the Mersey estuary and the sea. The city was now well and truly an inland port. Famously preceding that was the advent of rail transport – the Liverpool & Manchester Railway opening to the public in 1830. Even today, the scene from space is dominated by canals and rivers.

# Merseyside

## (Liverpool, Chester and The Wirral)

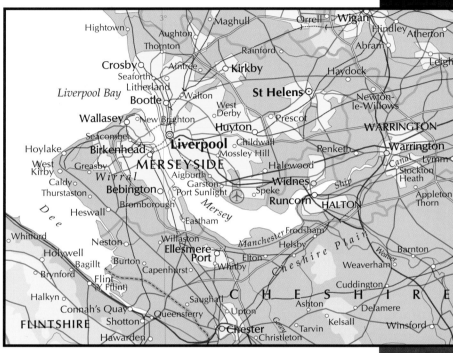

Liverpool's origins as a seaport date back many hundreds of years when it was the principal arrival and departure point for Ireland, a role it still maintains – albeit on a lesser scale. However, it was the opening up of the Americas and the associated trade in merchandise such as tobacco that brought about the city's heyday as a port. Nor was the trade just in commodities; the port has variously served as a place of slave importation and the traditional departure point of the great transatlantic liners. From a humble beginning in the early 18th Century when the first docks were built, the population of the city has increased more than eighty-fold to its current total of

half a million. This accounts for around one third of the population of Merseyside, the metropolitan county of approximately 647 square kilometres (250 square miles) whose towns include, among others, Birkenhead, Southport and St.Helens. Liverpool's prosperity spread to nearby areas, many of which became noted for their specialist industries. Birkenhead had shipbuilding; Widnes a long association with chemicals; Ellesmere Port, (served by the Shropshire Union Canal), was originally founded on the import of iron ore but is now noted for oil and petro-chemicals; while Bebington is famed both for soap and the 19th Century model housing village of Port Sunlight.

# The Lakes

## (The Lake District and Cumbria)

From its current ruggedness it is difficult to imagine that the Lake District was once a great dome comprised of a veritable mish-mash of limestone, slates and volcanic rocks. Their varying degree of erosive tolerance over millions of years has created the scenery we see today. Yet, additionally, there is probably nowhere else in Britain where the landscape has been so recently modified, for here ice has been at work. What once were steep v-shaped valleys were scoured by the glaciers of the last Ice Age to create today's broad, flat-bottomed valleys, some of which were dammed by glacial debris left by the retreating ice, resulting in the formation of the sixteen lakes that now make up the Lake District. The region's ancient dome shape is apparent from the layout of the lakes that, in their former guise of rivers, fanned out in an almost circular pattern centred midway between Helvellyn and the village of Grasmere. In all liklihood this was the dome's highest point, although the forces of erosion mean that the honour now falls to Scafell Pike, (pike is Old English for hill), which at 978 metres (3,210 feet) is the highest spot in England.

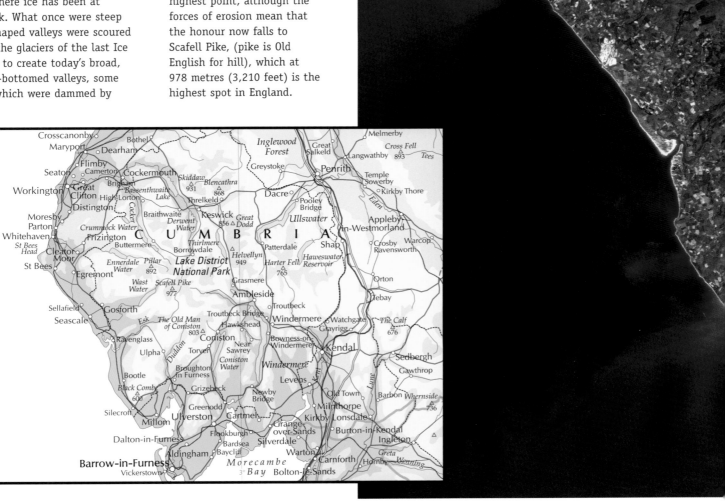

# Northumberland

## (The Cheviot Hills and Scottish Borders)

Northumberland is all that remains of the far larger Anglo-Saxon kingdom of Northumbria that stretched as far south as Humberside. For almost 48 kilometres (30 miles) the rolling Cheviot Hills form the natural border between England and Scotland, reaching their pinnacle at The Cheviot, a granite outcrop of some 815 metres (2,675 feet). The Cheviots in turn form part of the 1036 square kilometres (400 sq mile) Northumberland National Park, established in 1956. Within the park's boundaries lie two important man-made creations: Hadrian's Wall follows its southern periphery, surviving well in the vicinity of Haltwhistle, while Housesteads is the site of a fine preserved fort, one of many that were dotted along the wall's length. Kielder Water, meanwhile, is of more recent origin and in terms of volume is one of the largest man-made lakes in Europe. Most settlements are concentrated in the southeast of the region, principally around the Newcastle upon Tyne conurbation. Further north along the coast Holy Island, or Lindisfarne, temporarily surrenders its insular status each day to be connected to the mainland by a three mile causeway. Its status as one of Britain's early Christian sites dates back to a 7th Century monastery.

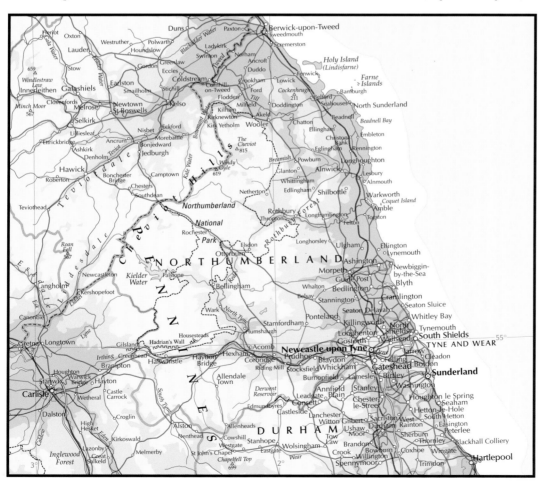

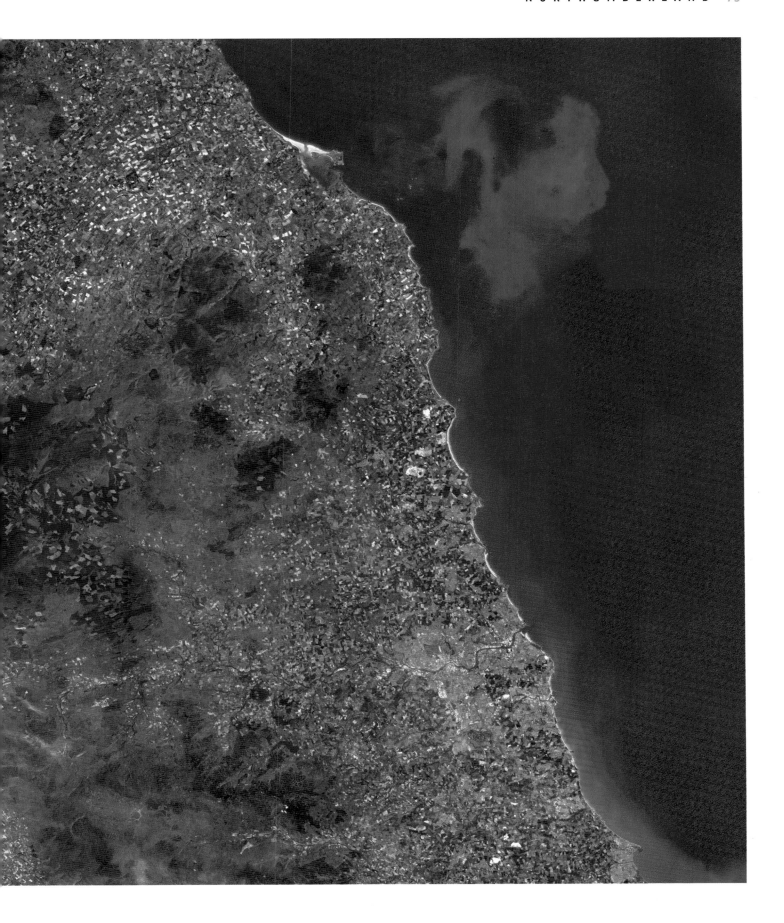

# Tyneside

## (Newcastle, Sunderland and Gateshead)

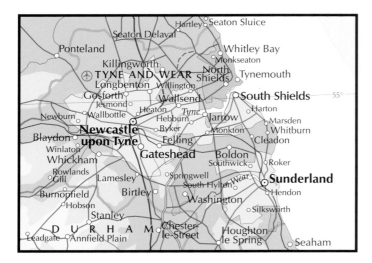

Geographically speaking, Tyneside is the industrial area lining the banks of the River Tyne downstream from the city of Newcastle upon Tyne. Divided into the metropolitan boroughs of North and South Tyneside, it is part of the metropolitan county of Tyne and Wear whose major towns comprise Newcastle, Sunderland, Gateshead and South and North Shields. The prosperity of the region was founded largely upon abundant supplies of coal which in turn were within easy access of the rivers and ports from which it could be exported to other parts of the UK. This readily available resource also attracted industry, principally ship building, (Sunderland was once the largest ship building town in the world), and, to a lesser degree, chemicals. The district's history, however, predates the Industrial Revolution by many hundreds of years. The Tyne and its estuary were traditionally guarded by the medieval castle at Tynemouth, which in turn was preceded by the Benedictine priory – burial place of the kings of the Saxon kingdom of Northumbria. Then remote, Tynemouth's population now exceeds 60,000. Wallsend, nearby, is so named because it marks the easternmost extremity of Hadrian's Wall. Bringing the story right up to date, Gateshead's Metro Centre is one of Europe's largest indoor shopping centres with covered malls totalling over 5 kilometres (3 miles) in length.

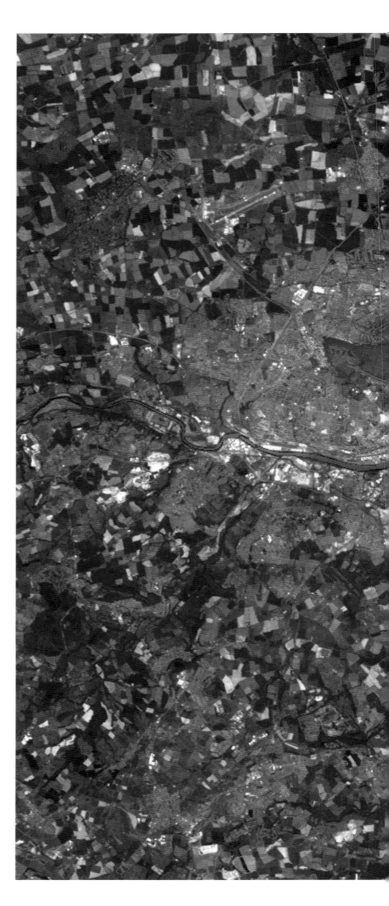

# Isle of Man

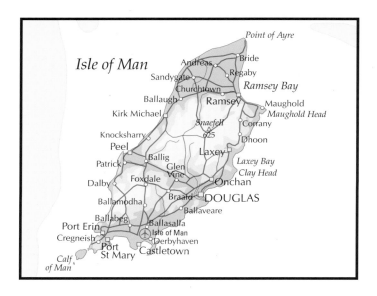

Set approximately the same distance from England, Scotland and Ireland, the Isle of Man probably became an island after the last Ice Age – only with the retreat of the ice and the ensuing rise in sea levels did it become independent of the mainland. This independence is maintained in more ways than one since the island is not officially part of the UK, but a Crown Dependency. In its time it has been ruled by England, Norway and Scotland; its ancient Gaelic name was Ellan Vannin which, reflecting its position in the middle of the Irish Sea, could possibly translate as "Central Island". It strongly retains its own variety of Gaelic culture, as well as the world's oldest parliament, the Tynwald. Geographically, the 570 square kilometre (220 square mile) island is comprised mainly of high ground. Particularly prevalent in the centre are slate outcrops which predominate and culminate in its highest point at Snaefell, 619 metres (2,030 feet) above sea level. Served by the famous Snaefell Mountain Railway, from here it is possible to see the coasts of England, Scotland, Ireland and Wales. Douglas, strung out along the shores of a bay with the same name, is the island's capital – a role acquired in the 19th Century from Castletown. The island's spectacular coastline, dominated by cliffs and bays, means that tourism is a big money spinner – as too is the offshore finance industry.

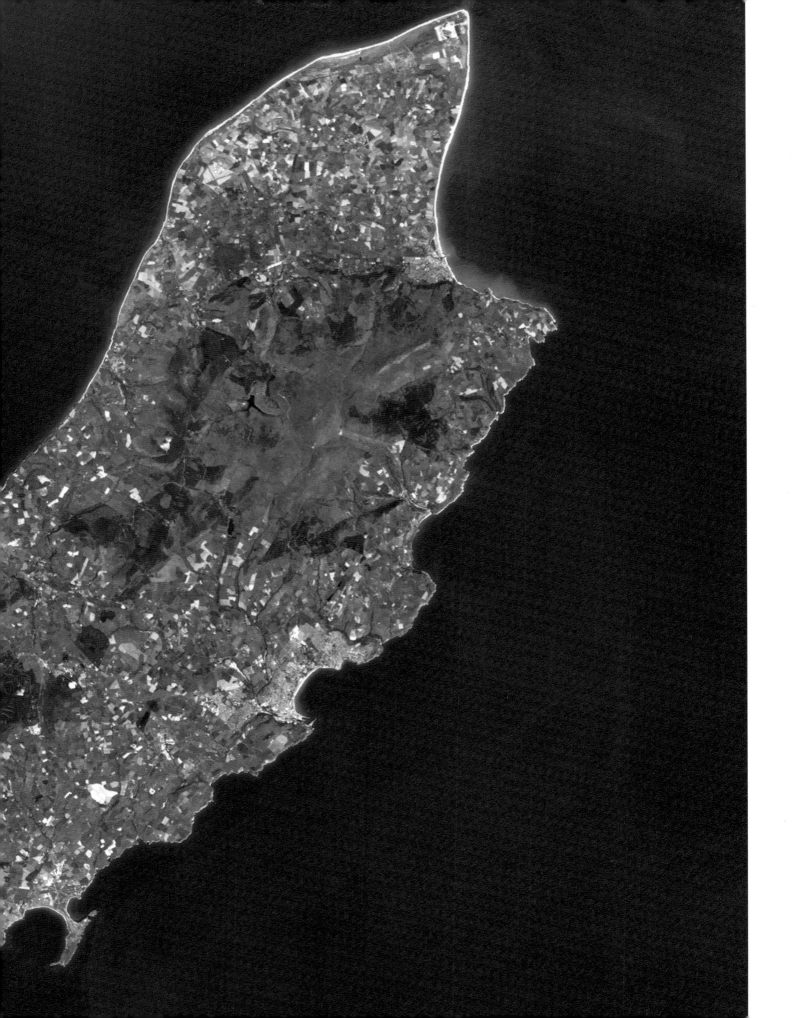

# Wales

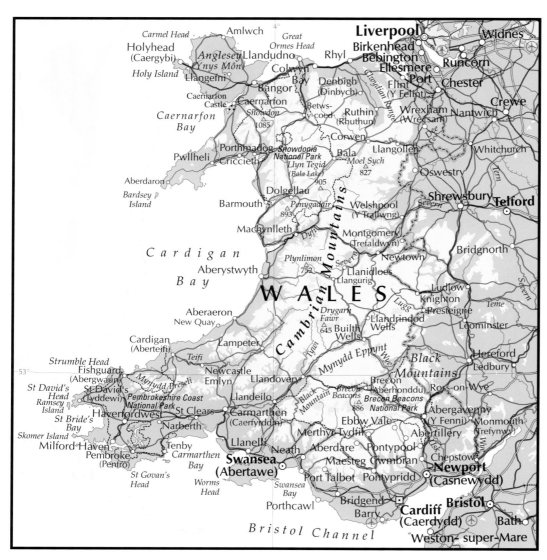

The hard volcanic rocks of the north; the limestone of the Gower Peninsula; the shales and sandstones of the south; their interaction with the earth's forces and the effects of nature have all helped to create the varied landscape that is Wales. Snowdonia and the Brecon Beacons are the principal features although equally important is the enormous semi-circular "dent" in which much of south Wales sits. The largely mountainous and upland nature of the Principality means that the main areas of habitation are on the coast, especially around the less harshly landscaped southern part of the country. Settlement here was also encouraged by the discovery of vast deposits of coal. Once the predominant employer, and famous the world over for its hard "Welsh Steam Coal", the mining industry has since shrunk dramatically. Ever since the Roman invasion, Wales has always aspired to a degree of autonomy – an ambition fulfilled at the end of the last Century with the founding of a National Assembly.

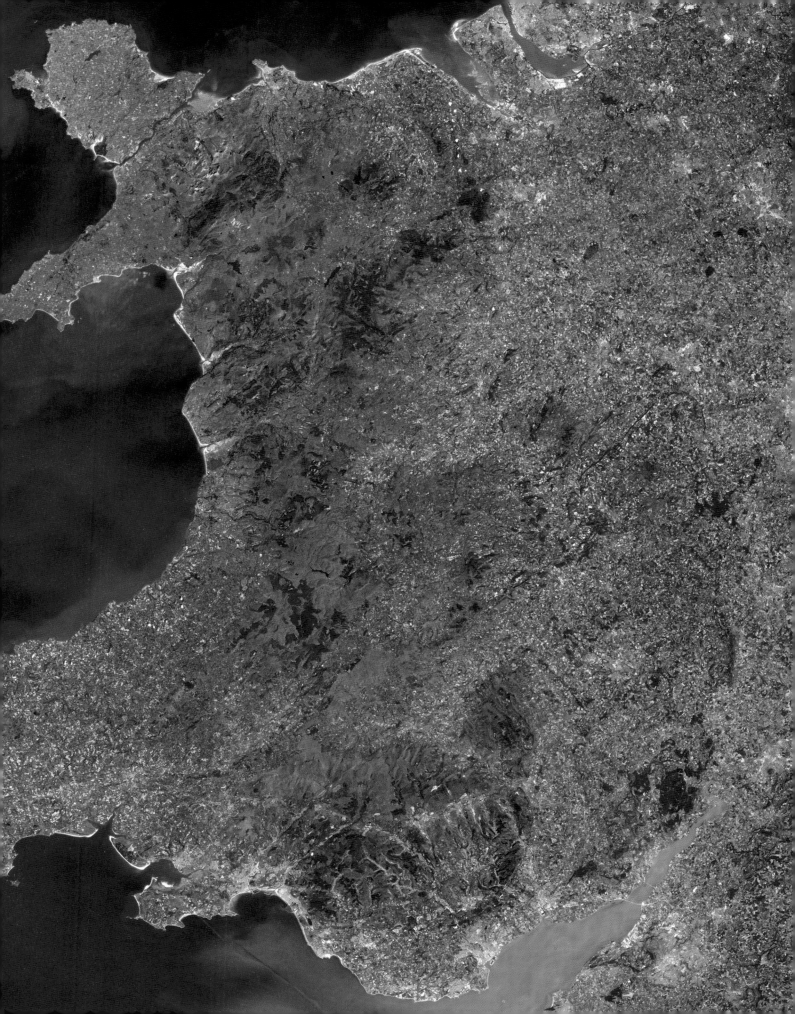

# The Valleys

## (The Welsh Valleys and the Gower )

The "dent" in which most of south Wales sits is readily apparent from this picture. Its physical form is stunningly revealed by the preponderance of rivers and associated valleys that radiate generally in a southerly direction from the uplands of the Brecon Beacons. Apart from the major coastal towns and cities, the linear nature of most settlements, (their development was severely restricted by the topography of the valleys), is also graphically illustrated. The region's one-time reliance upon the sea for trade is apparent from the preponderance of docks in Swansea, Cardiff, Barry and Port Talbot – all built to variously handle the import of ores and other cargoes,

and the export of Wales's greatest natural asset, coal. While coal is no longer of any great significance, Cardiff remains an important port for general merchandise, Swansea has adapted to handle petroleum products, while Port Talbot focuses on the bulk importation of iron ore. On a less industrialised note, the Gower Peninsula is a popular tourist destination and is characterised by its spectacularly rocky coast. In 1956 it became Britain's first Area of Outstanding Natural Beauty. Similarly, the Brecon Beacons were awarded National Park status in 1957. Extending over an area in excess of 1295 square kilometres (500 square miles), they lie almost entirely over 304 metres (1000 feet) above sea level.

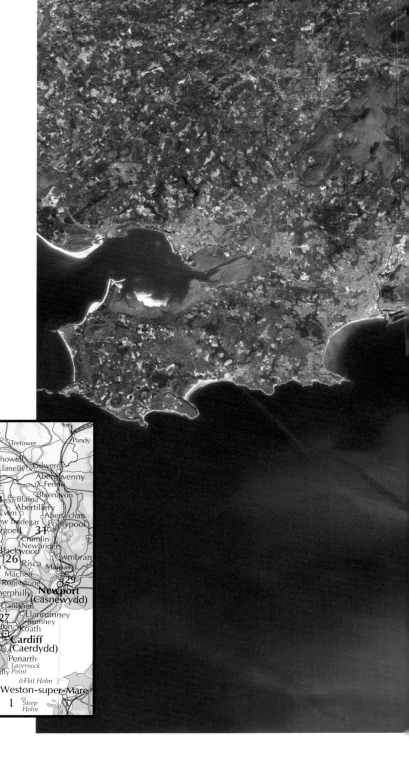

# Snowdonia

## (Conwy, Anglesey and the Menai Strait)

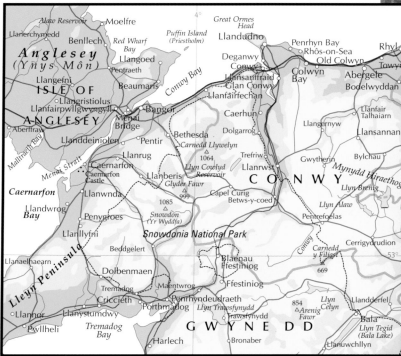

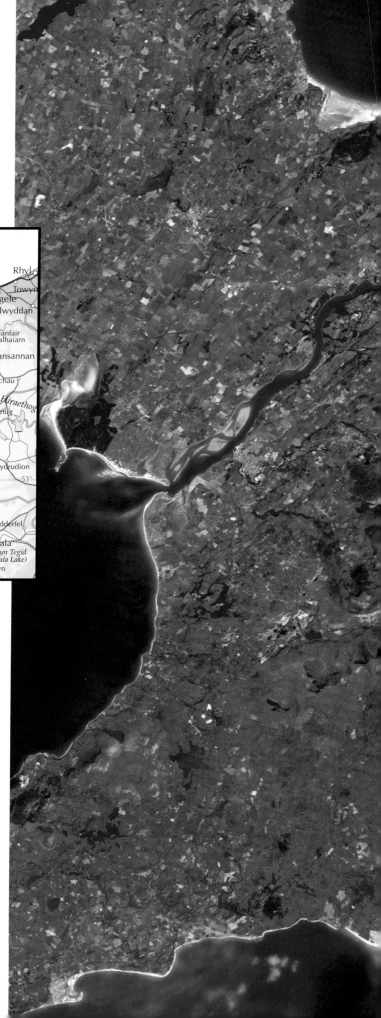

It is the relentless action of prehistoric ice sheets and glaciers upon hard-wearing ancient rocks that have resulted in the breath-taking scenery of Snowdonia. Covering over 2072 square kilometres (800 square miles) it became, in 1956, Wales's first and largest National Park, culminating in the country's highest peak, Mount Snowdon. The mountain's popularity with tourists is partly attributable to the opening in 1896 of the Snowdon Mountain Railway. Further south, particularly in the vicinity of Llanberis and Blaenau Ffestiniog, the landscape is pock-marked by huge slate quarries that in their heyday produced millions of roofing tiles. Once the principal employer of the region, production has now all but ceased. Of the natural lakes, the largest is Llyn Tegid, or Bala Lake, but a surprising number are man-made. Amongst them are Llyn Trawsfynydd, originally built for the generation of electricity, and Llyn Celyn. To the far north, the coastal landscape is generally less spectacular, although it rises in an almost unexpectedly dramatic fashion in the limestone headland of Great Orme's Head. The island of Anglesey is separated from the mainland by the Menai Strait which, in places, narrows to only a few hundred yards.

# Scotland

Physically, Scotland falls into a three way split: progressing from south to north – the Southern Uplands, the Central Lowlands and the Highlands and Islands. Ice has played a major role in sculpting the landscape, but Scotland also offers evidence of Britain's turbulent volcanic past as well as featuring some of its oldest rocks. It is a country of towering grandeur; a country that literally sheared in two through the geologic fault of the Great Glen; a land of mountains, rocky islands, vertiginous cliffs, craggy bays and desolate moorlands. Indisputably it is largely rural and isolated, (although there are several well-defined exceptions). Of the three countries that make up Great Britain, Scotland, at 77,694 square kilometres (30,000 square miles) accounts for about 33 per cent of its area yet is home to only 9 per cent of its population. Even the Romans failed to invade – indeed they did their best to keep the Scottish clans out of England by building Hadrian's Wall. For much of the period prior to the 18th Century Scotland was self-ruling. The 1707 Act of Union brought English and Scottish parliaments together until, at the end of the 20th Century, Scotland again had its own assembly. Most industry is limited to the Central Lowlands, although whisky distillation is more widespread.

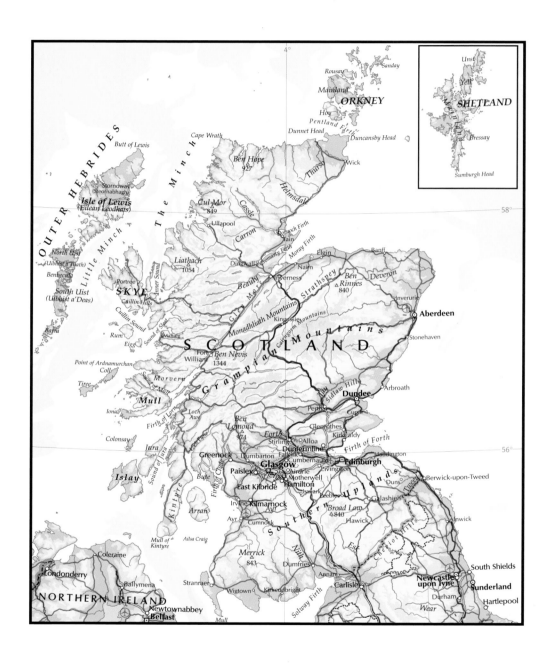

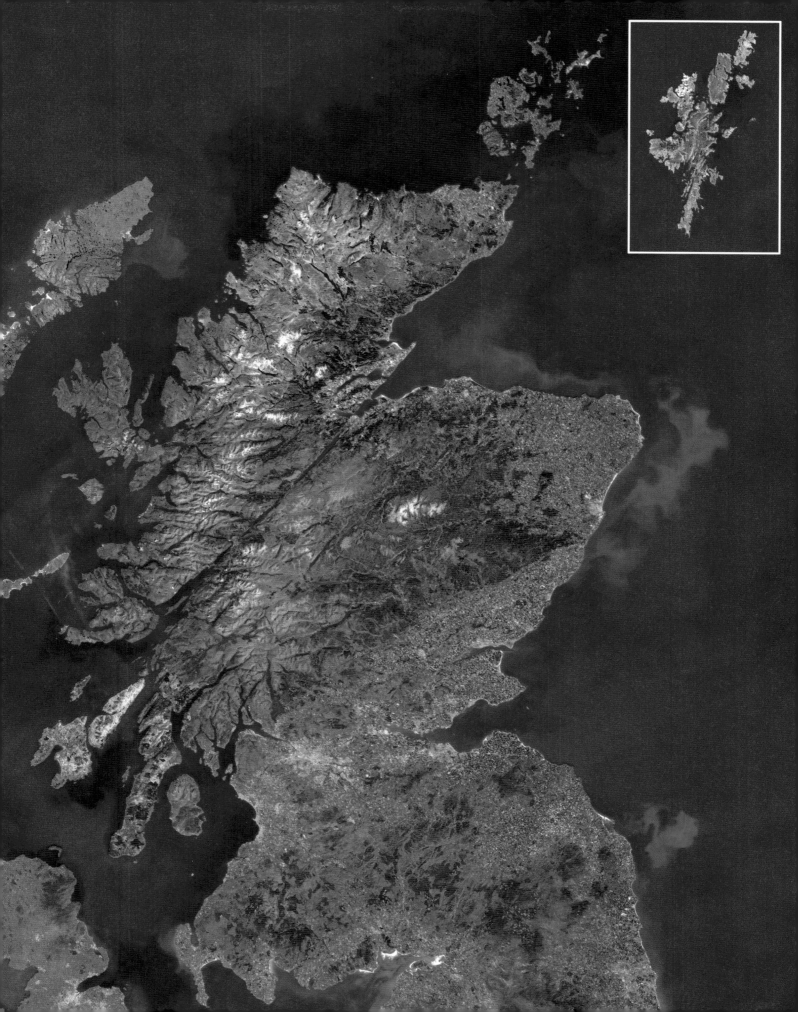

# The Firth of Forth

## (Edinburgh, Dunfermline and Fife)

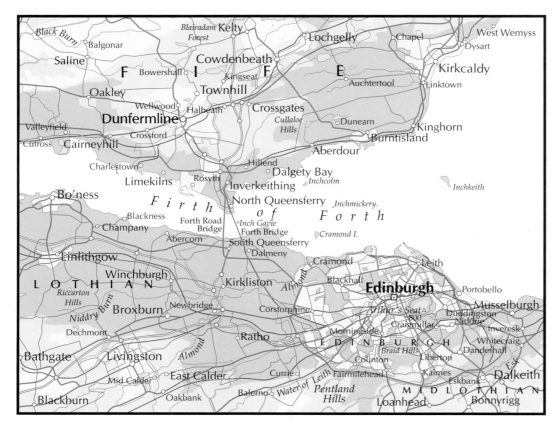

Of Nordic origin the word firth means a narrow sea inlet, or ria. The River Forth officially ends at Kincardine, just out of shot on this photograph, whereupon it enters the sea at the Firth of Forth which in its own right is 77 kilometres (48 miles) long. The Firth is only 27 kilometres (17 miles) shorter than the river and is a yawning 25.5 kilometres (16 miles) wide when it joins the North Sea. South Queensferry marks its narrowest point and as its name suggests, it was here that a long-established ferry connected Lothian with Fife. It followed that the spot was a natural candidate for a crossing of a more permanent nature, and accordingly a rail bridge was opened in 1890. Even now a tremendous engineering feat, 51,821 tonnes (51,000 tons) of steel were used to build the Forth Rail Bridge. It is 2.4 kilometres (1½ miles) long and is over 107 metres (350 feet) tall. Only in 1964 did a road bridge follow. On the Firth's southern shore lies Edinburgh, Scotland's capital city, a status once held by Dunfermline in whose cathedral are interred several ancient Scottish kings. On the north shore, just west of the road bridge, is the naval base of Rosyth.

# Edinburgh

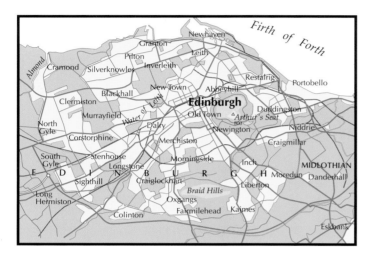

Edinburgh is where any doubt about Scotland's violent volcanic past can be allayed. On the eastern flank of the Old Town, Arthur's Seat at over 244 metres (800 feet) above sea level seems like any other hill; it is however, the remains of an extinct volcano. It sits in the middle of Holyrood Park, a large park set amid the bustling cityscape. Edinburgh's 11th Century castle, meanwhile, perches atop a mound of basalt. It is all that is left of a second volcano – its relatively softer cone having been worn away over millennia past to leave just the harder-wearing, long solidified, basalt plug. The city is divided into two geographic portions: the Old Town developed, naturally enough, around the castle – although there is evidence that a settlement existed here as early as the 6th or 7th Centuries. The New Town, which was built to the north of the Old, is something of a misnomer, being well over two hundred years of age. Edinburgh is a city of enormous character and vibrancy, and is famed as a long-established seat of learning. (Its university was founded in 1582.) Apart from the north, the city is surrounded on all sides by hills. Edinburgh's port, Leith, is now more noted for its leisure activities than any particularly large amount of maritime trade.

# Glasgow

Scotland's largest city, with a population of over 600,000, was probably founded in the 6th Century on a site where now stands the cathedral. Almost entirely ringed by hills, the landscape from space is dominated by Glasgow's principal geographic feature, the River Clyde – at 170.5 kilometres (106 miles), Scotland's third longest river. The city's role as a major port developed around 250 years ago, largely through the advent of trade with the Americas. The docks, particularly the square-shaped Prince's Dock on the river's south bank, show up especially well. Glasgow and its river also gained a reputation for ship-building, producing some of Britain's greatest vessels – the Queen Elizabeth among them. At one time, shipyards were

dotted for miles along the banks of the Clyde, Clydebank being home to the John Brown yard – perhaps the most famous of all. The city is also noted for having the most extensive underground railway outside of London, adoringly referred to as the Clockwork Orange because of the colour of the trains and the circular route they follow. Glasgow's old commercial centre on the Clyde's north bank is character-ised by the tightly crammed, criss-cross latticework of streets, although in recent years the city has marched incessantly westwards. Here many of its famed galleries and museums will be found. Glasgow Green, founded in 1662, is Britain's oldest municipal park and clearly shows lining the north bank of the river just prior to its first dive to the south.

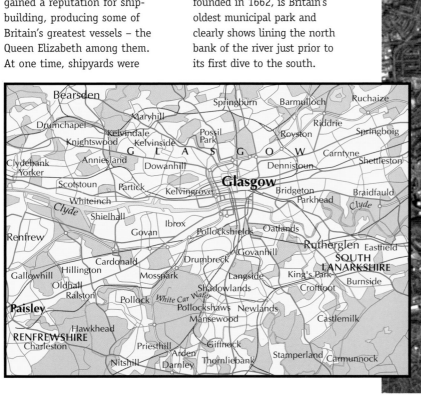

# Loch Lomond and The Trossachs

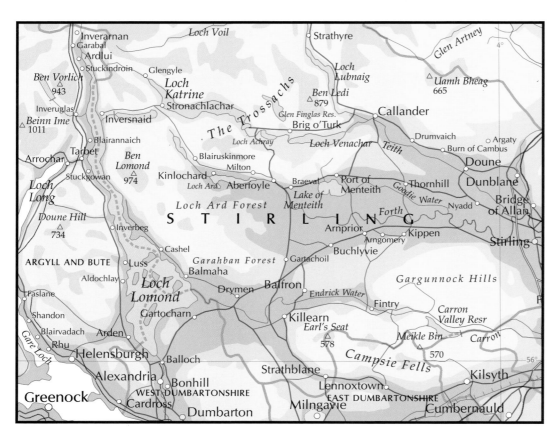

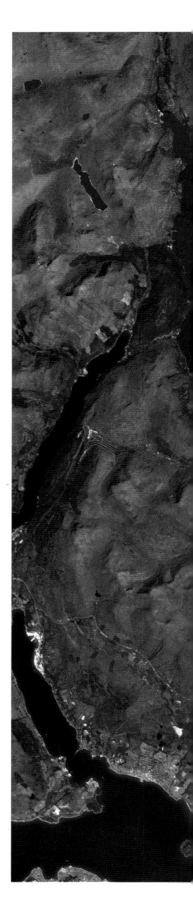

Loch Lomond is one of those splendid geographical oddities. There is nothing strange about it being Scotland's largest lake – sprinkled with islands, it is around 39 kilometres (24 miles) long and varies in width until it reaches about 8 kilometres (5 miles) in the south; the peculiarity is that in places the bottom of the loch plumbs depths in excess of 183 metres (600 feet), effectively making much of the loch bed several hundred feet below sea level. This is entirely attributable to the massive scouring effect of ice during the last Ice Age. Indeed, were it not for the narrow 8 kilometre (5 mile) wide strip of land around Alexandria, Loch Lomond would seemingly become part of the Firth of Clyde – albeit with a slight corresponding drop in water level. The low-lying nature of the loch is accentuated by the precipitous nature of the surrounding land, whose highest peak is Ben Lomond at 974 metres (3,195 feet). It is close to here that the headwaters of the River Forth rise. The Campsie Fells, to the south, are less dramatic in nature, while the Trossachs, draped in vegetation and woodland, were immortalised by Sir Walter Scott's *The Lady of the Lake*. (Trossachs translates literally as "bristly land".) Balloch is the principal town to serve the not inconsiderable influx of tourists to the area.

# Tayside

## (Dundee and Perth)

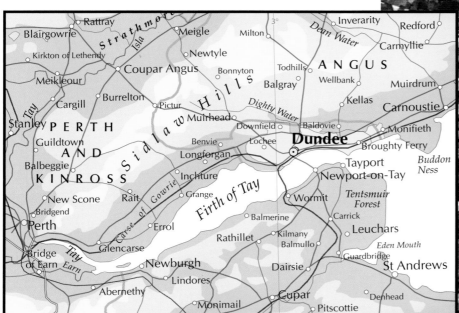

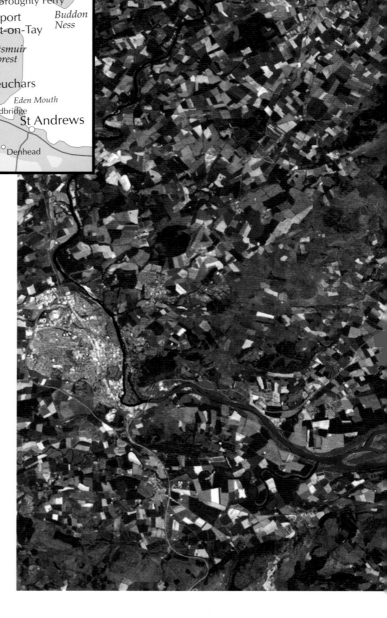

Tayside marks the northernmost boundary of the Central Lowlands. Comprised principally of glacial deposits, the ensuing fertile soil has made it one of Scotland's major producers of fruit and vegetables. For much of the Middle Ages Perth was Scotland's capital, while for many hundreds of years it marked the easternmost crossing of the River Tay, Scotland's longest river. Only in the 19th Century, with the advent of the railways, was an attempt made to bridge it further downstream at Dundee. The first Tay Bridge opened in 1877, but on 28th December 1879 it collapsed during a storm at the cost of seventy-five lives. It was not until 1887 that a replacement structure – still in use – was completed, and only in 1966 did a road bridge open, slightly further downstream. Dundee's docks, now used primarily for leisure purposes, serve as testimony that the city was once a great ship building centre. Captain Scott's *Discovery* was among the many vessels to be built here. On the southern side of the firth the broad sandy coastline is popular with many visitors and has given rise to numerous golf links, the most famous of which are at St. Andrews. The city's sporting fame is, however, but a recent innovation; more traditionally it is Scotland's oldest seat of learning, its first university being founded here in the 16th Century.

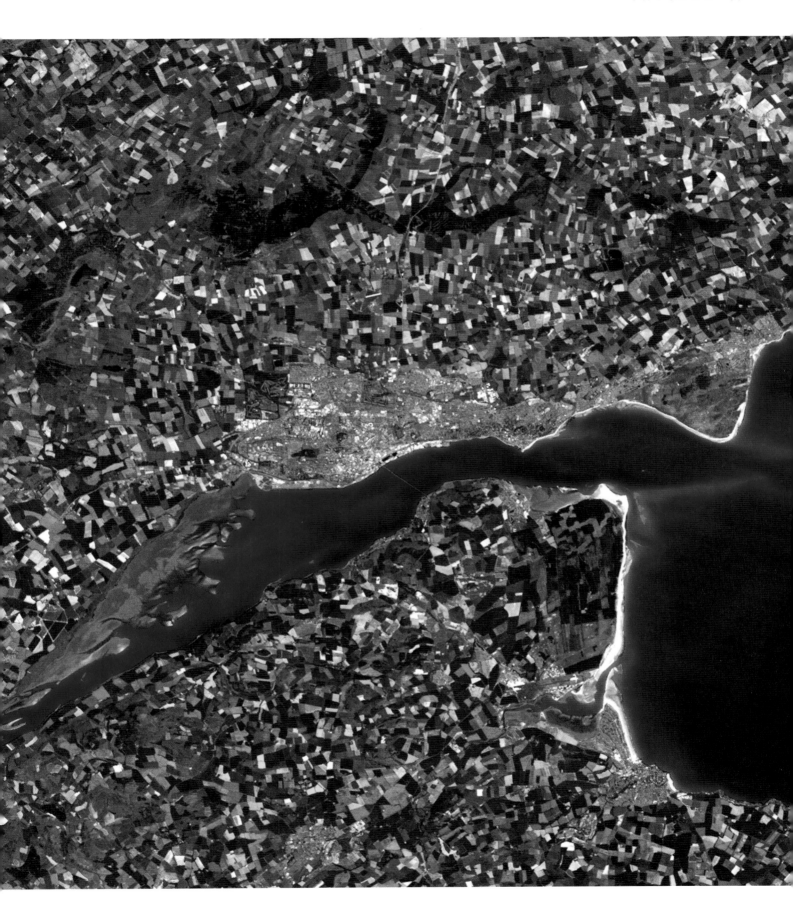

# Southern Hebrides

(Islay, Jura, Arran and Kintyre )

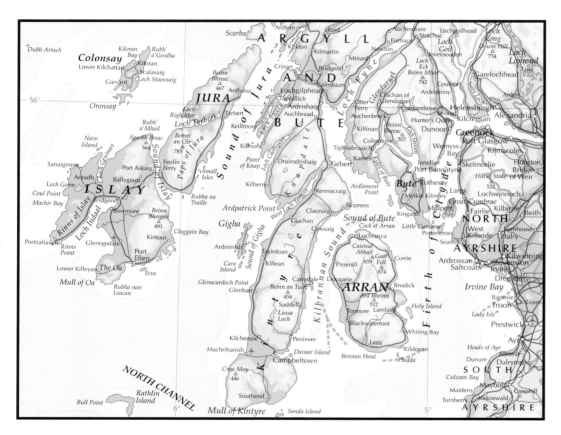

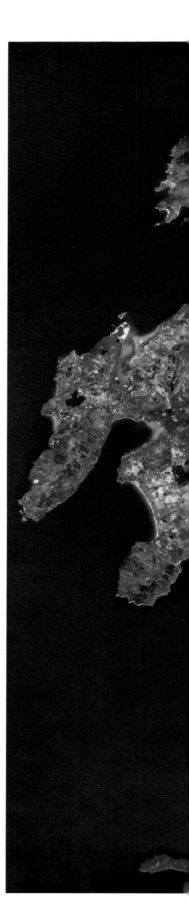

At well over 64 kilometres (40 miles), Kintyre is easily the longest peninsula in Scotland. But it was so very nearly much shorter in that it is almost severed at the village of Tarbert by the waters of West Loch Tarbert and Loch Fyne. (Tarbert is Gaelic for "isthmus" – into which category the village splendidly falls). Had the glacial melt waters risen just a little higher, Kintyre would surely have been an island. Campbeltown is the principal town of the peninsula which, at its southernmost tip is twice as far from the Scottish mainland as it is from the Irish. Rathlin Island is by tradition the place where Robert the Bruce sat in quiet contemplation with only the industrious spider for company. To the east of Kintyre, Arran is promoted as being "Scotland in miniature" – and not unreasonably so. Its 427 square kilometres (165 square miles) contain moors and fells, mountains and bays. The more spectacular scenery is on the north of the island, culminating in Goat Fell, a volcanic outcrop of over 853 metres (2,800 feet). Jura is by far the most rugged island of the district, and is the fourth largest of the Inner Hebrides. Its mountainous nature means that it revels in the luxury of just one road and that habitation is restricted to its south-east side. Islay, the largest island of the southern Hebrides is noted the world over for its malt whiskeys. Bowmore is its "capital".

# Mull and Ben Nevis

(Coll, Tiree and Fort William)

As mountains go, Ben Nevis, 1,343 metres (4,406 feet) and the highest in the British Isles, is almost an anti-climax. Despite its height, it lacks a peak in the traditional sense of the word and simply culminates in a level plateau. The general consensus is that this is attributable to the effect of ice during the Ice Age; if nothing else it dramatically demonstrates firstly how thick the ice was and secondly its enormous erosive power, vanquishing the peak that almost certainly once existed. Indeed, it is so level that the Victorians even managed to build an observatory on it. To the south, Loch Awe, at 40 kilometres (25 miles) in length, is Scotland's longest. It is overlooked by the 1,123 metres (3,685 feet) Ben Cruachan; outwardly it seems like any other of the region's numerous granite peaks, but

Ben Cruachan hides a surprise: buried within it is one of the world's largest hydro-electric power stations. Loch Linnhe, meanwhile, serves as a reminder that not all lochs hereabouts are freshwater. The island of Mull is another fine example of Scotland's volcanic past. It is almost entirely composed of ancient lava flows that once ran like rivers from the earth's crust. Despite this, the eastern part is fairly mountainous, with the western shoreline being more fjord-like in nature. The isle of Muck is one of immense beauty and comparatively good fertility.

# Skye

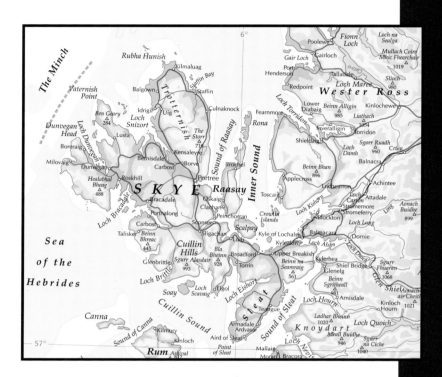

At almost 1813 square kilometres (700 square miles), Skye is the largest of the Inner Hebrides. In shape it is almost as though a giant has tightly squeezed a once rectangular island and placed it, in its new form, back into the ocean. Again, much of Skye's topography has developed as the result of ancient volcanic activity, although nothing more spectacular, probably, than enormous quantities of lava "leaking" through cracks in the earth's crust. The longevity of this activity is demonstrated in the Cuillin, (pronounced Coolin), Hills, whose highest point is Sgurr Alasdair at 993 metres (3,257 feet). Volcanic in nature, they are probably but a shadow of

their former selves having been subjected to serious erosion. For an island that is largely mountainous, the less dramatic southern area of Sleat, (pronounced Slate), is remarkably fertile. It is often referred to as The Garden of Skye. The island's capital, Portree, literally "King's Port", was so named after James V visited in 1540. Skye's most memorable event occurred in 1746 when, disguised as a woman, Bonnie Prince Charlie fled here with Flora MacDonald, eventually escaping to the mainland via Portree. In more recent times the Skye Bridge, clearly visible here, opened in 1995. Interestingly, the word "skye" is probably derived from the Nordic for... cloud.

# Loch Ness

## (Inverness and the Moray Firth)

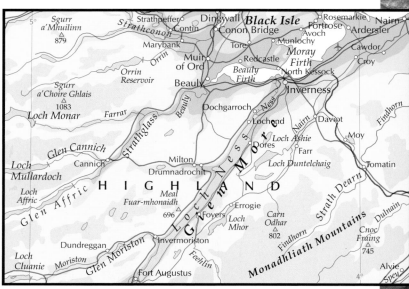

Doubtless on account of its famous "resident", Loch Ness at 35 kilometres (22 miles) in length and in places over 213 metres (700 feet) deep, unfairly upstages the far grander Great Glen, of which it makes up just one third. The Great Glen, or Glen More as it is occasionally called, runs the width of Scotland from Inverness on the east coast to Fort William on the west, and is a massive ancient geological fault, or rift, where the earth's crust literally sheared apart. The process, however, was not a sudden, violent action but prolonged over millions of years, probably starting around four hundred million years ago. More recent glaciation has accentuated its valley-like form, and three lakes have subsequently formed in it – of which Loch Ness is one. (The others are Loch Oich and Loch Lochy). The three were linked by Thomas Telford in the early 19th Century to form the Caledonian Canal, Fort Augustus – at the southern extremity of Loch Ness – being home to a series of canal locks. Inverness, population 40,000, is the principal centre of population; it is capital of the Highlands and connected to Loch Ness by both the Caledonian Canal and the River Ness. To the south, the city is flanked by the inhospitable but scenically spectacular Monadhliath Mountains while on the northern shore of the Moray Firth, the Black Isle is a peninsula of relatively low-lying, fertile agricultural land.

# Orkney

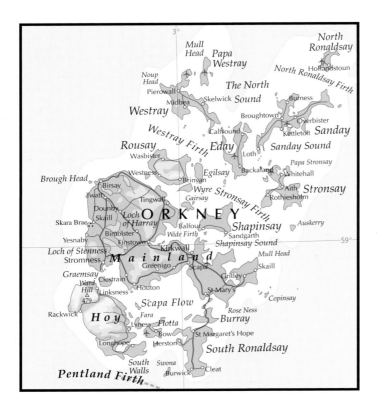

Fewer than 20,000 people live on the ninety-plus islands that make up Orkney, the southern-most of which is just a few miles from the Scottish mainland. For all that, they remain a world apart; indeed, until the late 16th Century they fell under Scandinavian rule. Mainland is the principal island, and it is here that Kirkwall, the capital, is situated. Of all the islands Hoy, the second largest, is probably the most spectacular with towering cliffs and, inland, Ward Hill – the Orkneys' highest point at 478.5 metres (1,570 feet). It is separated from Mainland by Scapa Flow, a surprisingly deep area of water that was used as an anchorage in both World Wars. It was here that the German fleet was notoriously scuttled in 1919, and where the Royal Oakl was sunk in 1939. The Churchill Barriers, a man-made causeway linking Mainland and South Ronaldsay, were subsequently built in an effort to seal off Scapa Flow, at least from the east. Orkney also boasts what is probably more evidence of prehistoric habitation than anywhere else in Britain – there are numerous standing stones, ancient settlements and Neolithic burial chambers. Two of the most notable are the tomb of Maes Howe and the Ring of Brodgar, both on Mainland. These, together with the islands' bountiful and varied wildlife, attract thousands of visitors each year.

# Shetland

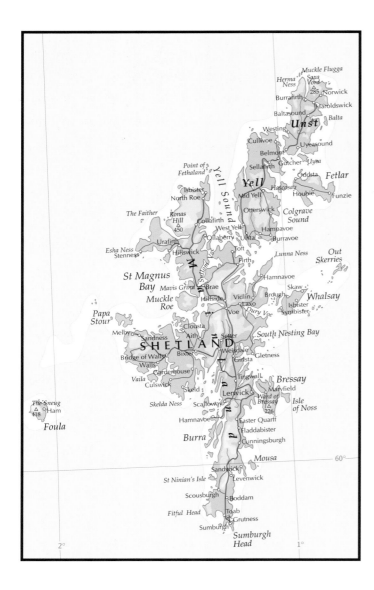

And so our journey through the British Isles brings us to their northernmost extremity – Shetland, more than one hundred islands and islets of which only a small percentage is inhabited by the population of 24,000. Of these almost one third live in Lerwick, the islands' capital, on the principal island of Mainland and the most northerly town in Britain. Fishing and agriculture are traditionally the main employers, but the discovery of North Sea oil in the vicinity led the area to enjoy a renaissance after many years of population decline. The oil terminal of Sullom Voe, on Mainland's northern tip, is one of the largest in Europe; even from space its form is unmistakable. Shetland also bristles with evidence of prehistoric civilisation: there are several brochs, (small, stone, Iron Age forts), of which the best preserved is on Mousa, a small island just east of Mainland; Jarlshof is an important Bronze Age site on the far south of Mainland. The ancient volcanic rocks, the incessant forces of sea and wind, and the abrasive might of long-disappeared ice, (the melting of which probably "created" many of the islands), have collectively spawned Shetland's wild and craggy, landscape. The charmingly named Muckle Flugga appears to be the most northerly point of the British Isles; but that honour befalls Out Stack, a rocky outcrop just beyond.

# Ireland

In some respects the geology and topography of Ireland is little more than a continuation of that on the opposite shore of the Irish Sea, the ingress of the ocean being a fairly recent feature in the geological time scale. However, there are major differences, not least through the effects of glacial deposits and the actions of ice, which have altered the landscape dramatically. Thus, while limestone may be an extremely prevalent "natural" bedrock, (which in central Ireland it certainly is), enormous expanses are hidden beneath deposits of clays and peat. This is largely attributable to millions of years of deposition and the fact that Ireland was smothered by ice during the Ice Age. The end result is the country's infamous peat bogs and a land of great fertility. In a nutshell, the central part of Ireland is level and low-lying in nature, while the coastal fringes are often mountainous, (with some notable exceptions), with granite and sandstone peaks either thrust skywards by the collision of ancient continents or, as in the north, the incessant escape of lava. The Atlantic coast is more scenically spectacular, Carrantuohill being Ireland's highest point at just over 1036 metres (3,400 feet). Of the land mass, the Republic makes up 43,451 kilometres (27,000 square miles), while Northern Ireland is just over 12,949 square kilometres (5,000 square feet).

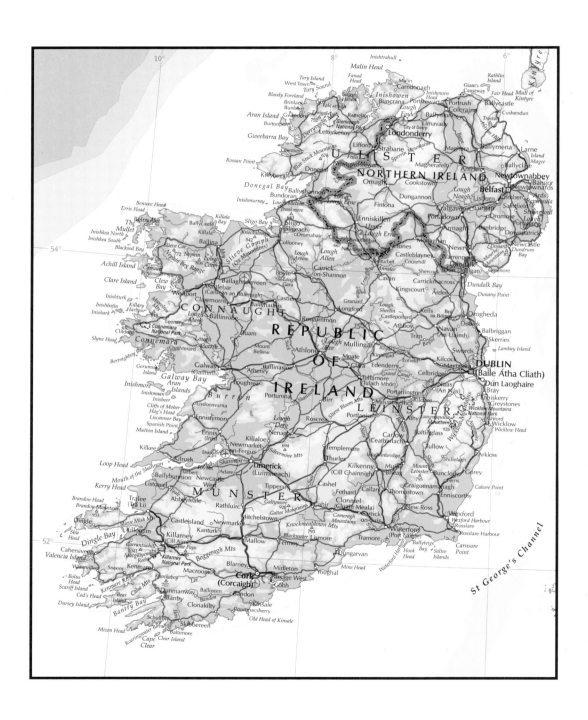

# Ulster

Whilst in modern parlance the term Ulster is usually taken to mean Northern Ireland, geographically speaking it also includes the counties of Donegal, Cavan and Monaghan in the Republic. It is a region whose bedrock is largely volcanic in nature, especially in the east – attributable to the massive welling up and subsequent outpouring of molten rock – rather like dozens of enormous saucepans gently boiling over. The legacy of this spell of instability remains today in Antrim's cliffs and the columns of the Giant's Causeway, its basalt "frozen" at the very spot where it was forced, at

tremendous pressure, through the earth's surface. Here too is evidence that the geology is but a continuation of that in Scotland: similar columns can be found on Staffa. The most noticeable geographic feature is Lough Neagh which, with an area in excess of 388 square kilometres (150 square miles), is the biggest, (and a contender for the shallowest), lake in the British Isles. It is accentuated by the surrounding Antrim Hills, the Sperrin Mountains and the Mourne Mountains. Slieve Donard, in the Mourne Mountains, forms Northern Ireland's highest point at 852 metres (2,795 feet).

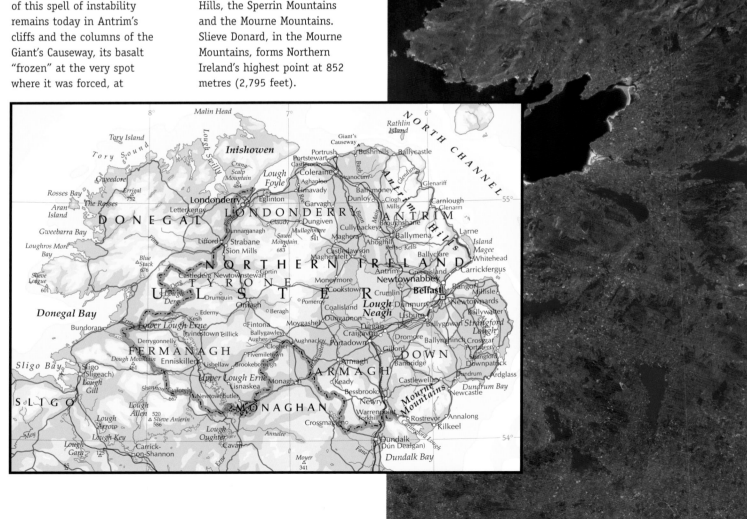

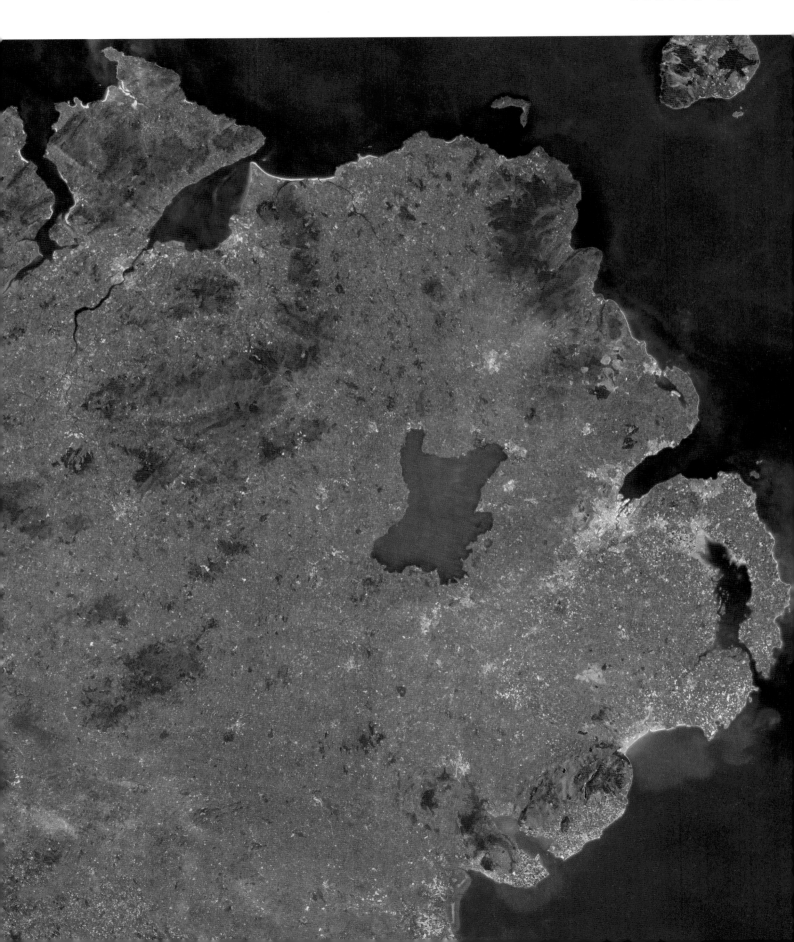

# Belfast

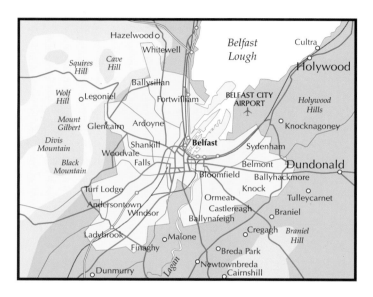

Clustered around the shores of Belfast Lough, and sidling inland along the banks of its river, the Lagan, the city of Belfast is home to almost 300,000 people. Apart from the lough, the city is surrounded by high ground, so it perhaps comes as something of a surprise that much of it is built on land reclaimed from the sea. Belfast's history extends back to the 12th Century when the first castle was built, but industrially its reputation was originally built on linen manufacture – by the 17th Century the city had acquired a reputation as one of the greatest producers in the world. It was around this time that Belfast's importance as a port was established, the deep waters of the lough making it an ideal site. By the 18th Century a ship building industry had developed, (the first yard opened in 1791), and by the time of the Industrial Revolution, the ship building yards of Belfast were the envy of the world. The tradition continues today, albeit on a far lesser scale; even so, the city is still home to the largest dry dock in the world, and it has maintained its role as a gateway to Northern Ireland with regular ferry services to England, Scotland and the Isle of Man. A more recent arrival, (1938), is the City Airport, built on the docks' eastern flank and showing splendidly on the photograph. One of the earliest "city" airports, it was originally partially operated by Harland & Wolff who branched out into aircraft manufacture, in addition to the ships for which they remain world-famous.

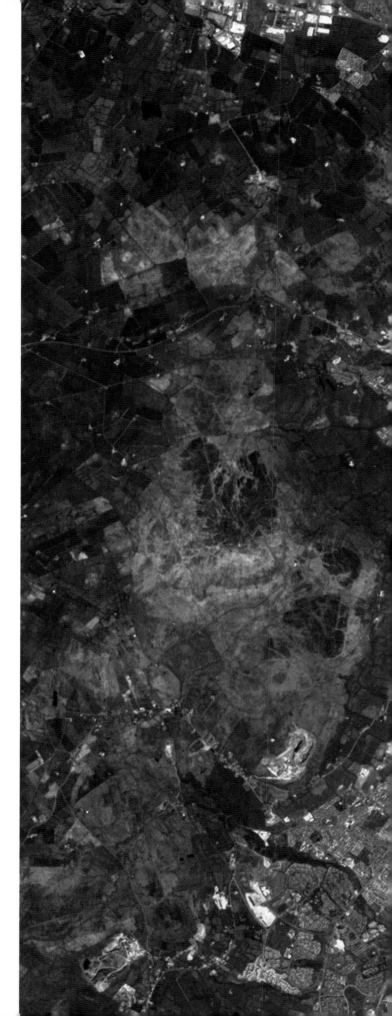

# Dublin

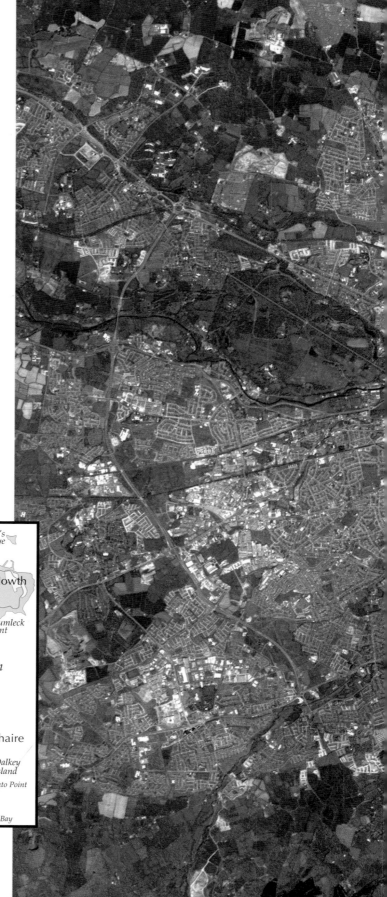

With its wide sweeping bay offering a safe, natural harbour, and the famous River Liffey opening up the interior, it is hardly surprising that the site of Dublin has been occupied since at least Viking times. Several man-made features show extremely well on the photograph, not least the port area on the river estuary and the harbour arms of Dun Laoghaire embracing a large area of Dublin Bay. However, the most unusual of all is North Bull Island, whose elongated form straddles the bay's northern periphery. It started life humbly in the 19th Century as a breakwater built to deflect silt away from the harbour. It has evidently worked supremely well – to the extent that with the aid of nothing more than marine drift it has metamorphosed into a fully-fledged island complete with golf course, (for which a little help was required from man). Surrounding physical constraints in the form of the Irish Sea and the Wicklow Mountains mean that any expansion of Dublin has been severely restricted, but even so in the 18th Century it had the second highest population of any city in the Empire. Nevertheless, it remains one of Europe's most compact capitals, an attribute meaning that it is possible for visitors to "do" the whole of Dublin in a relatively short time. This and the rejuvenation of the city in the 1990s have made it one of the most popular city-break destinations from the UK in recent years.

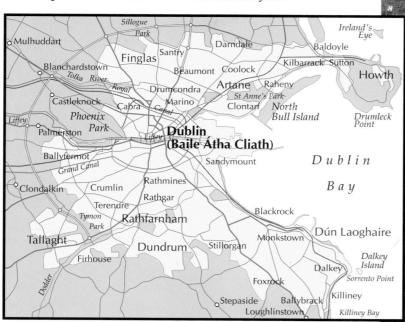

# Kerry

Lain down millions of years apart, layers of sandstone and limestone were thrown into turmoil when ancient continents collided, forming the base ingredients of Kerry's dramatic scenery. The hard, sandstone mountains and hills, typified by the Macgillycuddy Reeks, contrast starkly with less resistant limestone valleys, which in turn have occasionally been inundated by the sea – sometimes in spectacular fashion. What now appear as bays started life as nothing more than river valleys. The mountainous areas show well on the photograph, and are accentuated by the abrupt cessation of the lower-lying agricultural land north of Killarney, and Tralee – Kerry's capital – in the northwest. Otherwise, the unforgiving nature of the terrain has effectively restricted human habitation to small centres on the coast. Indeed, the area is of such beauty that tourists must outnumber the indigenous population many times over each year. Valencia Island to the south of Dingle Bay on the southwest coast lost some of its former remoteness when it acquired a road bridge to the mainland in 1971. However, well before that it had staked its own little claim to fame as a place featured in the Shipping Forecast. It falls within the much wider-reaching sea area of Shannon.

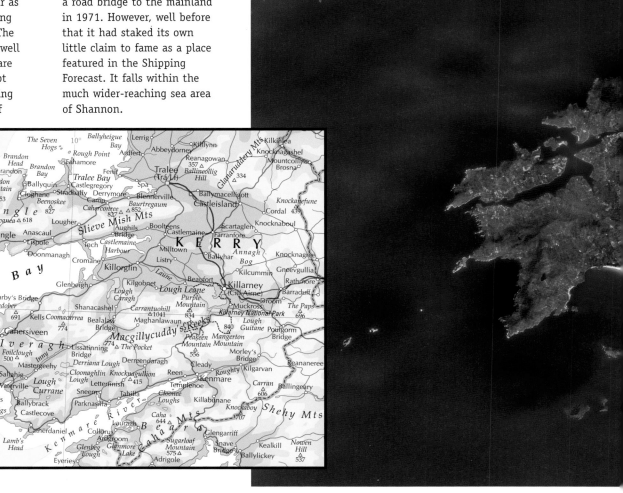

# Index

A
Abberton Reservoir 36, 40
Abbeydorney 118
Abbeyfeale 110
Abbeyhill 90
Abbots Langley 32, 39
Abbots Leigh 20
Abbotsbury 18
Aberaeron 80
Aberaman 82
Abercanaid 82
Abercorn 88
Abercynon 18, 82
Aberdare 80, 82
Aberdaron 80
Aberdeen 12, 86
Aberdour 88
Aberffraw 84
Aberford 58
Aberfoyle 94
Abergavenny (Y Fenni) 80, 82
Abergele 84
Abergwaun (Fishguard) 80
Aberhonddu (Brecon) 80
Aberkenfig 18, 82
Abernethy 96
Abersychan 82
Abertawe (Swansea) 12, 80, 82
Aberteifi (Cardigan) 80
Abertillery 80, 82
Aberystwyth 12, 80
Abingdon 39
Abram 66, 70
Accrington 56, 66
Acharacle 100
Achill Island 110
Achintree 102
Achnacroish 100
Achosnich 100
Ackworth Moor Top 58
Acock's Green 50
Acomb 74
Acton 36, 40
Adare 110
Adderbury 39
Addlestone 30, 32
Adlington 66
Adrigole 118
Adwick le Street 56
Aghanloo 112
Agnagar Bridge 118
Ahogill 112
Aigburth 70
Ailsa Craig 86
Aintree 70
Aird of Sleat 102
Airdrie 86
Aire, R. 58
Airedale 56, 58
Aith, Shetland 108
Aith, Stronsay 106
Akeld 74
Alaw Reservoir 84
Albaston 14, 16
Aldbourne 22
Alde, R. 40
Aldeburgh 40
Aldenham 32, 39
Alderbury 18, 22
Alderholt 18, 22
Aldershot 22, 30
Aldingham 66, 72
Aldington 28
Aldochlay 94
Aldridge 49
Alexandria 94, 98
Alford 54, 56
Alfreton 46
Allendale Town 74
Allenheads 74
Allerton 58
Allhallows 28
Alloa 86
Alloway 98
Almond, R. 88, 90
Almondsbury 18, 20
Alnmouth 74
Alnwick 74, 86
Alresford 36, 40
Alston 74
Alton 22, 26
Altrincham 66, 68
Alveston 18
Alvie 104
Amble 74
Amblecote 49
Ambleside 72
Ambrosden 39
Amersham 39
Amesbury 18
Amlwch 80
Ammanford 82
Amport 22
Ampthill 39, 46
An Nâs (Naas) 110

An Uaimh (Navan) 110
Anascaul 118
Ancaster 54
Ancroft 74
Ancrum 74
Andersontown 114
Andover 22
Andreas 78
Anglesey (Ynys Môn) 12, 80, 84
Angmering 26
Anlaby 64
Annagh Bog 118
Annalee, R. 110, 112
Annalong 112
Annan 86
Annfield Plain 74, 76
Anniesland 92
Ant, R. 40
Antrim 110, 112
Antrim Hills 110, 112
Aomach Buidhe 102
Aonach air Chrith 102
Aoradh 98
Appleby-in-Westmorland 72
Applecross 102
Appledore, Devon 16
Appledore, Kent 26, 28
Appleton Thorn 66, 70
Aran Island, Ulster 110, 112
Aran Islands, Galway Bay 110
Arbroath 86
Ard Bheinn 98
Ardchiavaig 100
Ardee 110
Arden, Glasgow 92
Arden, Loch Lomond 98
Ardentinny 98
Ardersier 104
Ardfern 98
Ardfert 118
Ardglass 112
Ardgroom 118
Ardlamont Point 98
Ardleigh 36, 40
Ardlue 94
Ardlussa 98
Ardminish 98
Ardmolich 100
Ardmore Point 100
Ardnamurchan 100
Ardoyne 114
Ardpatrick Point 98
Ardrishaig 98
Ardrossan 98
Ards Peninsula 110
Ardtoe 100
Ardvasar 102
Arenig Fawr 84
Argaty 94
Argyll and Bute 94, 98
Arinagour 100
Arklow 110
Arlesey 39, 40
Arlham 34
Armagh 12, 110, 112
Armdale 102
Arne 18
Arngomery 94
Arnisdale 102
Arnold 46
Arno's Vale 20
Arnprior 94
Arran 12, 86, 98
Arran Islands 12
Arrochar 94
Artane 116
Arthur's Seat 88, 90
Arundel 26
Ascot 22, 30
Ash, Kent 28
Ash, Surrey 22, 30
Ashburton 16, 18
Ashchurch 39
Ashcott 18
Ashdown Forest 26
Ashford 18
Ashford, Hants. 22
Ashford, Kent 26, 28
Ashford, Middx. 30, 32
Ashford, Rep. of Ireland 110
Ashill 40
Ashkirk 74
Ashley 40
Ashrington 74
Ashton 70
Ashton Canal 68
Ashton upon Mersey 68
Ashton-under-Lyne 52, 68
Ashurst, Hants. 22
Ashurst, Kent 26, 30
Ashwick 18
Askival 102
Aston 50
Aston Clinton 39
Athboy 110
Athenry 110
Atherington 16
Atherstone 46, 49

Atherton 66, 70
Athlone 12, 110
Athy 110
Attadale 102
Attleborough 40
Attlebridge 40
Auchbraad 98
Auchenbreck 98
Auchindrain 98
Auchtertool 88
Audenshaw 68
Augher 112
Aughils Bridge 118
Aughnacloy 112
Aughton, Lancs. 66, 70
Aughton, Yorks. 60
Auskerry 106
Avebury 18, 22
Aveley 32, 36
Avoch 104
Avon, R. 16, 18, 20, 22, 46
Avonmore, R. 110
Avonmouth 18, 20
Axe, R. 16, 18
Axminster 16, 18
Aycliffe 56
Aylesbury 39
Aylesford 28
Aylesham 28
Aylsham 40, 42
Ayr 12, 86, 98
Ayr, R. 86

B
Babbacombe Bay 16, 18
Backaland 106
Backwell 18
Bacup 66
Baggy Point 16
Bagilt 70
Bagshot 22, 30
Baguley 68
Baildon 58
Baile Atha Cliath (Dublin) 12, 110, 116
Bain, R. 54
Bainahard 100
Bala 80, 84
Bala Lake (Llyn Tegid) 80, 84
Balbeggie 96
Balbriggan 110
Balcombe 26
Balderton 54
Baldovie 94
Baldoyle 116
Baldslow 26, 28
Balemartine 100
Balern 88
Balfour 106
Balfron 94
Balgonar 88
Balgown 102
Balgray 96
Balham 34
Ballabeg 78
Ballachulish 100
Ballaghaderreen 110
Ballamodha 78
Ballasalla 78
Ballaugh 78
Ballaveare 78
Ballig 78
Ballina 110
Ballinasloe 110
Ballincollig Hill 118
Ballineen 110
Ballingeary 118
Ballinrobe 110
Ballinskelligs 118
Ballinskelligs Bay 118
Balloch 78
Ballybrack, Dublin 116
Ballybrack, Kerry 118
Ballybunnion 110
Ballycastle 110, 112
Ballyclare 110, 112
Ballydavid Head 118
Ballyfermot 116
Ballyferriter 118
Ballygawley 112
Ballygowan 112
Ballygrant 98
Ballyhackmore 114
Ballyheigue Bay 118
Ballyhar 118
Ballylickey 118
Ballymacelligott 118
Ballymena 86, 110, 112
Ballymoney 110, 112
Ballynafeigh 114
Ballynahinch 112
Ballyquin 118
Ballyshannon 110
Ballysillan 114
Ballyteige Bay 110
Ballywalter 112
Balmacara 102

Balmaha 94
Balmerine 96
Balmullo 96
Balnacra 102
Balta 108
Baltasound 108
Baltimore 110
Baltinglass 110
Balvicar 100
Bamburgh 74
Bamingham 40
Bampton, Devon 16, 18
Bampton, Oxon. 39
Banbridge 110, 112
Banbury 39, 46
Bandon 110
Bandon, R. 110
Banff 86
Bangor, N.Ireland 110, 112
Bangor, Wales 80, 84
Banham 40
Bann, R. 110, 112
Banstead 30, 32
Bantham 16
Bantry 110
Bantry Bay 110
Banwell 18
Bar Hill 40
Barassie 98
Barbon 72
Bardney 54
Bardsea 72
Bardsey Island 80
Bargoed 82
Barham 28
Barkway 36, 40
Barle, R. 16, 18
Barley 36, 39, 40
Barmouth 80
Barmulloch 92
Barnard Castle 56
Barnes 34
Barnet 32, 39
Barnoldswick 66
Barnsley 52, 56, 60
Barnstaple 16
Barnstaple Bay see Bideford Bay
Barnton 70
Barra, Is. 86
Barraduff 118
Barrapoll 100
Barrow 110
Barrow Gurney 20
Barrow, R. 110
Barrow upon Humber 54, 64
Barrow-in-Furness 66, 72
Barrowby 54
Barrowford 66
Barry 18, 80, 82
Barton 54, 66
Barton Broad 42
Barton-le-Clay 39
Barton-upon-Humber 54, 56, 64
Basildon 36
Basingstoke 22
Bassenthwaite Lake 72
Bassett 36
Bassingbourn 36, 40
Bassingham 54
Bath 12, 18, 80
Batheaston 18
Bathford 18
Bathgate 88
Batley 58
Battersea 34
Battersea Park 34
Battle 26, 28
Baughurst 22
Baurtregaum 118
Bawdeswell 40
Bawdsey 36, 40
Bawtry 56
Bay Head 118
Baycliff 72
Beachy Head 26
Beaconsfield 39
Beadnell 74
Beadnell Bay 74
Bealalaw Bridge 118
Beaminster 18
Bear Island 110
Bearsden 92
Bearsted 28
Bearwood 50
Beauchief 60
Beaufort 118
Beauly 104
Beauly Firth 104
Beauly, R. 86, 104
Beaumaris 84
Beaumont 116
Bebington 66, 70, 80
Beccles 40, 42
Bedale 56
Beddau 18, 82
Beddgelert 84

Beddingham 26
Bedford 46
Bedford Levels 40, 44
Bedlington 74
Bedminster 20
Bedwas 18, 82
Bedworth 49
Beenoskee 118
Beer 16, 18
Beeston 46
Beetley 40
Beighton 60
Beinn Alligin 102
Beinn an Oir 98
Beinn an Turc 98
Beinn Bhan 102
Beinn Bheigeir 98
Beinn Bhreac 98, 100, 102
Beinn Bhuidhe 100
Beinn Ime 94
Beinn Mhor 98
Beinn na Seamraig 102
Beinn Sgritheall 102
Beinn Sgulaird 100
Beith 98
Belfast 12, 86, 110, 112, 114
Belfast City Airport 114
Belfast Lough 114
Belford 74
Bellingham 74
Belmont, Belfast 114
Belmont, Yell 108
Belmullet 110
Belsay 74
Belton 40, 42
Belturbet 110
Bembridge 22, 24
Ben Buic 100
Ben Cruachan 100
Ben Geary 102
Ben Hiant 100
Ben Hope 86
Ben Ledi 94
Ben Lomond 86, 94
Ben More 100
Ben Nevis 12, 86, 100
Ben Rinnes 86
Ben Starw 100
Ben Vorlich 94
Benbecula 86
Benenden 26, 28
Benllech 82
Benn Resipol 100
Bennan Head 98
Benson 39
Bentley 60
Benvie 96
Benwee Head 110
Beragh 112
Bere Alston 14, 16
Bere Ferrers 14, 16
Bere Regis 18
Berinsfield 39
Berkeley 18
Berkhamsted 39
Berkshire Downs 22
Berkswell 49
Bermondsey 34
Bernisdale 102
Berrow 18
Berry Head 16
Bertraghbow Bay 110
Berwick-upon-Tweed 74, 86
Bessacarr 60
Bessbrook 112
Bethersden 26, 28
Bethesda 84
Bethnal Green 34
Betws-y-coed 80, 84
Beult, R. 26, 28
Beverley 56
Bewl Water 26, 28
Bexhill 26
Bheag 110
Bibury 39
Bicester 39
Bickenhill 49
Bickleigh, N.Devon 16, 18
Bickleigh, S.Devon 14, 16
Bicknacre 36
Biddenden 26, 28
Bidean nam Bian 100
Bideford 16
Bideford Bay 16
Bienn Chapull 100
Big o'Turk 94
Bigbury Bay 16
Biggin Hill 30, 32
Biggleswade 40
Bill of Portland 18
Billericay 36
Billinghay 54
Billingshurst 26
Billockby 40, 42
Bilton 56, 64
Bimbister 106
Binbrook 54
Binbrook 54

Bingley 56, 58
Binnein Mor 100
Birch 68
Birchfield 50
Birchington 28
Birkenhead 66, 70, 80
Birmingham 12, 46, 49, 50
Birr 110
Birsay 106
Birtle 74, 76
Bishop Auckland 56
Bishop's Cleeve 39
Bishop's Hull 16, 18
Bishop's Lydeard 16, 18
Bishop's Stortford 36, 40
Bishop's Tawton 16
Bishop's Waltham 22
Bishopsteignton 16, 18
Bishopsworth 20
Bisley 39
Bitton 18, 20
Bixter 108
Bla Bheinn 102
Black Burn, R. 88
Black Combe 66, 72
Black Down Hills 16, 18
Black Head 14
Black Hill 52, 56
Black Isle 104
Black Mountain 114
Black Mountains, Wales 80, 82
Black Notley 36, 40
Blackadder Water 74
Blackburn, Lancs. 56, 66
Blackburn, Scotland 88
Blackfield 22, 24
Blackhall 88, 90
Blackhall Colliery 74
Blackheath 34
Blackmoor Gate 16
Blackness 88
Blackpool 12, 66
Blackrock 116
Blacksod Bay 110
Blackwater, R. 36
Blackwater (Rep. of Ireland), R.110
Blackwater (Ulster), R. 12, 112
Blackwaterfoot 98
Blackwood 18, 82
Blaenau Ffestiniog 84
Blaenavon 82
Blaengarw 18, 82
Blaengwrach 82
Blagdon 18
Blaich 100
Blaina 82
Blairadam Forest 88
Blairannaich 94
Blairgowrie 96
Blairuskinmore 94
Blairvadach 94
Blakeney 40
Blakeney Point 40
Blanchardstown 116
Blandford Camp 18
Blandford Forum 18
Blarney 110
Blasket Sound 110
Blaydon 74, 76
Blean 28
Blencathra 72
Blenheim Palace 39
Blennerville 118
Bletchley 39, 46
Blewbury 39
Blockley 39
Bloody Foreland 110
Bloomfield 114
Bloxham 39
Blue Stack 112
Blue Stack Mts 110
Blyth 60, 74
Blyth, R. 40
Blyton 54
Boddam 108
Bodelwyddan 84
Bodicote 39
Bodmin 14
Bodmin Moor 14
Boggeragh Mts 110
Bognor Regis 22, 26
Boldon 74, 76
Boldre 22, 24
Bollington 52
Bolt Head 16
Boltby 63
Bolton 56, 66
Bolton-le-Sands 66, 72
Bolus Head 110, 118
Bolventor 14, 16
Bonawe 100
Bonchester Bridge 74
Bo'ness 88
Bonhill 94
Bonjedward 74
Bonnyrigg 88
Bonnyton 96
Boolteens 118
Bootle 66, 70, 72
Boreham 36
Borehamwood 32, 39
Boreraig 102
Borough Green 28
Borrowdale 72
Borve 102
Boscastle 14
Bosham 22, 26
Boston 40, 54
Botesdale 40
Bothel 72
Bothenhampton 18
Bottesford 54, 56, 64
Boulsworth Hill 66

Bournbrook 50
Bourne 40
Bournemouth 12, 18, 22
Bourton 18
Bourton-on-the-Water 39
Bovey, R. 16, 18
Bovey Tracey 16, 18
Bovington Camp 18
Bow 106
Bow Creek 34
Bowburn 74
Bowershall 88
Bowmont Water 74
Bowmore 98
Bowness-on-Windermere 72
Box 18
Boyle 110
Boyne, R. 110
Braald 78
Bracadale 102
Bracebridge Heath 54
Brackley 39
Bracknell 22, 30
Bracora 102
Bradford 56, 58
Bradford-on-Avon 18
Brading 24
Bradley 64
Bradley Stoke 20
Bradninch 16, 18
Bradpole 18
Bradshaw 66
Bradwell 52
Bradwell Waterside 36
Brae 108
Braeval 94
Braid Hills 88, 90
Braidfauld 92
Braintree 36, 40
Braithwaite 72
Bramford 36, 40
Bramley 60
Brampton, Cambs. 40
Brampton, Cumbria 74
Brampton, Suffolk 40
Brancaster 40
Brandon 118
Brandon Bay 118
Brandon, Durham 74
Brandon Head 110, 118
Brandon Mts 110, 118
Brandon, Norfolk 40
Braniel 114
Braniel Hill 114
Bransgore 18, 22
Branston 54
Brantham 36, 40
Bratton 18
Braunton 16
Bray 22
Bray, R. 16, 18
Bray, Rep. of Ireland 110
Breage 14
Breamish, R. 74
Breckland 40
Brecon (Aberhonddu) 80
Brecon Beacons 80, 82
Brecon Beacons National Park 80, 82
Breda Park 114
Bredbury 68
Brede, R. 26, 28
Bredon 39
Brendon Hills 16, 18
Brent Knoll 18
Brent Reservoir 34
Brentwood 32, 36
Bressay 86, 108
Breydon Water 42
Bride 78
Bridge 28
Bridge of Allan 94
Bridge of Earn 96
Bridge of Walls 108
Bridge of Weir 98
Bridgend, Islay 98
Bridgend, Scotland 96, 98
Bridgend, Wales 18, 80, 82
Bridgeton 92
Bridgewater Canal 68
Bridgnorth 46, 80
Bridgwater 16, 18
Bridgwater Bay 16, 18
Bridlington 56
Bridlington Bay 56
Bridport 18
Brigg 54, 56, 64
Brigham 72
Brighouse 58
Brighstone 24
Brightlingsea 36, 40
Brighton 12, 26
Brinlack 110
Brinyan 106
Brislington 20
Bristol 12, 18, 20, 80
Bristol Channel 12, 18, 20, 80
Bristol International Airport 18
Briston 40
Brit, R. 18
Brixham 16
Brixton 34
Broad Law 86
Broad Oak 26, 28
Broadclyst 16, 18
Broadford 102
Broadheath 68
Broadmayne 18
Broadstairs 28
Broadway 39
Broadwey 18
Broadwindsor 18
Brochel 102
Brock, R. 66
Brockenhurst 22, 24

Brockley 34
Brockwell Park 34
Brockworth 39
Brodick 98
Bromborough 70
Bromham 18
Bromley, E.London 34
Bromley, S.London 30, 32
Brompton 63
Bromsgrove 46
Bronaber 84
Brooke 40, 42
Brookeborough 112
Broomfield 36
Broomhead Reservoir 52
Brosna 118
Brotton 63
Brough 54, 56, 64
Brough Head 106
Brough, Whalsay 108
Broughshane 112
Broughton 54, 64
Broughton in Furness 72
Broughton Park 68
Broughtown 106
Broughty Ferry 96
Brownhills 49
Broxburn 88
Brú na Bóinne 110
Brue, R. 18
Brundall 40, 42
Brundish 40
Bruton 18
Brynamman 82
Brynford 70
Buchlyvie 94
Buckden 40
Buckfastleigh 16
Buckingham 39
Bucklebury 22
Buddon Ness 96
Bude 14, 16
Bude Bay 14
Budleigh Salterton 16, 18
Bulford 18, 22
Bulkington 49
Bull Point 98
Bulmer Tye 36, 40
Bunbeg 110
Bunclody 110
Buncrana 110
Bundoran 110, 112
Bungay 40, 42
Buntingford 39, 40
Burbage 18, 22
Bure, R. 40, 42
Bures 36, 40
Burford 39
Burgess Hill 26
Burgh le Marsh 54
Burghclere 22
Burghfield Common 22
Burley 18, 22
Burn of Cambus 94
Burnage 68
Burness 106
Burnham 22
Burnham Market 40
Burnham-on-Crouch 36
Burnham-on-Sea 16, 18
Burnhouse 98
Burniston 63
Burnley 56, 66
Burnopfield 74, 76
Burnside 92
Burntisland 88
Burra 108
Burrafirth 108
Burravoe 108
Burray 106
Burrelton 96
Burren 110
Burry Inlet 82
Burry Port 82
Burscough 66
Burstow 26, 30
Burton, Bournemouth 18, 22
Burton Bradstock 18
Burton, Merseyside 70
Burton upon Stather 54
Burton upon Trent 46
Burton-in-Kendal 66, 72
Burtonport 110
Burwash 26, 28
Burwell 40
Burwick 106
Bury 56, 66
Bury St Edmunds 40
Bush, R. 112
Bushey 32, 39
Bushmills 112
Busk 68
Bute 86, 98
Butt of Lewis 86
Buttermere 72
Buxted 26
Buxton 46
Byfleet 30, 32
Byker 76
Bylchau 84

C
Cadbury Heath 20
Caddington 39
Caerau 18, 82
Caerdydd (Cardiff) 12, 18, 80, 82
Caerfyrddin (Carmarthen) 12, 80, 82
Caergybi (Holyhead) 80
Caerhuno 80
Caerleon 18
Caernarfon 12, 80, 84
Caernarfon Bay 80, 84

Caernarfon Castle 80, 84
Caerphilly 82
Caerwent 18
Caha 118
Caha Mts. 110, 118
Caherconree 118
Cahersiveen 110, 118
Cahir 110
Cahore Point 110
Cairnbaan 98
Cairndow 100
Cairneyhill 88
Cairngorm Mts. 86
Cairnshill 114
Caisleán an Bharraigh 110
Caisteal Abhail 98
Caister-on-Sea 40, 42
Caistor 54, 56
Calder, R. 58
Caldew, R. 74
Caldicot 18
Caldy 70
Calf of Man 78
Calfsound 106
Calgary 100
Calgary Bay 100
Caliach Point 100
California 50
Callan 110
Callander 94
Calliford Reservoir 14
Callington 14, 16
Calne 18
Calver 52
Cam, Glos. 18, 39
Cam, R. 40
Camasnacroise 100
Camberley 22, 30
Camberwell 34
Camborne 14
Cambrian Mts 12, 80
Cambridge 12, 40
Camden 34
Camelford 72
Camp 118
Campbeltown 98
Campsie Fells 94
Camptown 74
Canna 102
Cannich 104
Cannington 16, 18
Cannock 46
Cannock Chase 46
Canonbie 74
Canterbury 28
Canton 18, 82
Canvey Island 36
Caolas 100
Cape Clear 110
Cape Cornwall 14
Cape Wrath 12, 86
Capel Curig 84
Capel, Kent 28
Capel le Ferne 28
Capel St Mary 36, 40
Capel, Surrey 26, 30
Capenhurst 70
Cara Island 98
Carbost 102
Cardiff (Caerdydd) 12, 18, 80, 82
Cardiff International Airport 18, 82
Cardigan (Aberteifi) 80
Cardigan Bay 12, 80
Cardonald 92
Cardross 94
Carforth 56
Cargill 96
Carington Reservoir 46
Carlingford Lough 112
Carlisle 12, 74, 86
Carlow (Ceatharlach) 110
Carlton 58
Carlton Colville 40, 42
Carlton in Lindrick 56
Carmarthen Bay 80
Carmarthen (Caerfyrddin) 12, 80, 82
Carmel Head 80
Carmunnock 92
Carmyllie 96
Carn Odhar 104
Carndonagh 110
Carnedd Llywelyn 84
Carnedd y Filiast 84
Carnforth 66, 72
Carnlough 112
Carnoustie 96
Carnsore Point 110
Carntyne 92
Carradale 98
Carran 118
Carrantuohill 12, 110, 118
Carrick 96
Carrick-on-Shannon 110, 112
Carrick-on-Suir 110
Carrickfergus 112
Carrickmacross 110
Carrington 68
Carron, R. 86, 94
Carron Valley Reservoir 94
Carsaig 100
Carse of Gowrie 96
Carterton 39
Cartmel 66, 72
Cashel, Stirling 94
Cashel, Rep. of Ireland 110
Casnewydd (Newport) 12, 18, 80, 82
Cassle, R. 86
Castle Bromwich 49
Castle Carrock 74
Castle Cary 18
Castlebar 110
Castleblayney 110
Castlecove 118
Castledawson 112

Castlederg 112
Castleford 56, 58
Castlegregory 118
Castleisland 110, 118
Castleknock 116
Castlemaine 118
Castlemaine Harbour 118
Castlemilk 92
Castlepollard 110
Castlerea 110
Castlereagh 114
Castlerock 112
Castleside 74
Castleton 63
Castletown 78
Castlewellan 112
Catcliffe 60
Caterham 30, 32
Catford 34
Catherdaniel 118
Cathrain 20
Caton 66
Catterick 56
Cavan 12, 110, 112
Cave Hill 114
Cawdor 104
Cawston 40
Caythorpe 54
Cayton 56, 63
Ceatharlach (Carlow) 110
Celbridge 110
Cerphilly 18
Cerrigydrudion 84
Chad Valley 50
Chadderton 68
Chagford 16, 18
Chailey 26
Chale 24
Chalgrove 39
Champany 88
Channel Tunnel 28
Chapel 88
Chapel Allerton 58
Chapel St Leonards 54
Chapel-en-le-Frith 46, 52, 56
Chapelfell Top 74
Chapeltown 60
Chard 16, 18
Chardstock 16, 18
Charfield 18
Charing 28
Charlbury 39
Charleston 92
Charlestown 88
Charlton, Hants. 22
Charlton, Wilts. 18, 39
Charlton Kings 39
Charlwood 26, 30
Charminster 18
Charmouth 16, 18
Chartham 28
Chatham 28
Chatteris 40, 44
Chatton 74
Cheadle 66, 68
Chedburgh 40
Cheddar 18
Chelmer, R. 36, 40
Chelmsford 36
Chelsea 34
Cheltenham 39
Chepstow 18, 80
Cheriton 22
Cherry Willingham 54
Chertsey 30, 32
Cherwell, R. 39
Chesham 39
Cheshire Plain 46, 70
Cheshunt 32, 36
Chesil Beach 18
Chester 12, 46, 70, 80
Chester-le-Street 74, 76
Chesterfield 46
Chesters 74
Chetham Hill 68
Cheviot Hills 74, 86
Chew Magna 18
Chew Valley Lake 18
Chichester 22, 26
Chickerell 18
Chiddingford 26, 30
Chieveley 22
Chigwell 32, 36
Chilcompton 18
Childrey 39
Childwall 70
Chilham 28
Chiltern Hills 39
Chingford 32, 39
Chinnor 39
Chippenham 18
Chipping Campden 39
Chipping Norton 39
Chipping Ongar 32, 36
Chipping Sodbury 18
Chiseldon 18, 22
Cholsey 39
Chorley Ramsbottom 66
Chorleywood 39
Christchurch 18, 22
Christleton 70
Christon Bank 74
Chudleigh 16, 18
Chulmleigh 16, 18
Church End 36
Churchfield 50
Churchtown 78
Cill Airne (Killarney) 110, 118
Cill Chainnigh (Kilkenny) 12, 110
Cilybebyll 82
City of Derry Airport 110
Clabhach 100
Clachan 98, 100, 102
Clachan of Glendaruel 98

Clacton-on-Sea 36, 40
Cladich 100
Claggain Bay 98
Claonaig 98
Clapham Common 34
Clara 110
Clare 36, 40
Clare Island 110
Clare, R. 110
Claremorris 110
Claudy 112
Clavering 36, 40
Clay Head 78
Claydon 40
Claypole 54
Clayton 26
Clayton-le-Moors 66
Cleadon 74, 76
Cleady 118
Clear Island 110
Cleat 106
Cleator Moor 72
Clekheaton 58
Clemiston 90
Clestrain 106
Clevedon 18
Cleveland Hills 56, 63
Clevelys 66
Clew Bay 110
Clifden 110
Clifford 110
Clifton, Beds. 39, 40
Clifton, Bristol 20
Clitheroe 66
Clogh Mills 112
Cloghane 118
Clogher 112
Clonakilty 110
Clondalkin 116
Clones 110
Clonmel (Cluain Meala) 110
Clontarf 116
Cloonaghlin Lough 118
Cloonee Loughs 118
Cloughton 63
Clousta 108
Clovelly 16
Clovenfords 74
Clovullin 100
Cluain Meala (Clonmel) 110
Clutton 18
Clwydian Range 80
Clydach 82
Clydach Vale 18, 82
Clyde, R. 92
Clydebank 92
Clynacartan 118
Cnoc Fraing 104
Cnoc Moy 98
Coalisland 112
Coalpit Heath 20
Coalville 46
Cóbh 110
Cobham 30, 32
Cock of Arran 98
Cockenheugh 74
Cockermouth 72
Cockett 82
Cod Beck, R. 63
Coddenham 40
Codicote 39, 40
Cod's Head 110
Codsall 49
Coggeshall 36, 40
Colchester 36, 40
Colden Common 22
Coldstream 74
Cole, R. 50
Coleford 18
Colen, R. 36
Coleraine 12, 86, 110, 112
Colerne 18
Coleshill 49
Colgrave Sound 108
Colinton 88, 90
Colintraive 98
Coll 86, 100
Collafirth 108
Collingham 54
Collooney 110
Collorus 118
Coln, R. 39
Colnbrook 30, 32
Colne 56, 66
Colne, R. 40
Colney Heath 39
Colonsay 86, 98
Coltishall 40, 42
Colwyn Bay 80, 84
Colyford 16, 18
Colyton 16, 18
Combe Martin 16
Combe St Nicholas 16, 18
Comber 110
Comberton 40
Comeragh Mts 110
Congdon's Shop 14, 16
Congleton 46
Congresbury 18
Coningsby 54
Conisbrough 56, 60
Coniston 72
Coniston Water 72
Connah's Quay 70
Connel 100
Connemara 110
Connemara National Park 110
Conon Bridge 104
Consett 74
Constantine 14

Contin 104
Conwy 84
Conwy Bay 84
Conwy, R. 84
Cookham 39
Cookstown 110, 112
Coolock 116
Coomacarrea 118
Coombe 14, 16
Coombe Bissett 18, 22
Cootehill 110
Copinsay 106
Copplestone 16, 18
Copthorne 26, 30
Copythorne 22
Coquet Island 74
Corbridge 74
Corby 46
Corcaigh (Cork) 12, 110
Cordal 118
Cordat 118
Corfe Castle 18
Corfe Mullen 18
Cork (Corcaigh) 12, 110
Cornhill-on-Tweed 74
Cornwall 14
Corpach 100
Corrany 78
Corraun Peninsula 110
Corrie 98
Corringham 36
Corsham 18
Corstorphine 88, 90
Corton 40, 42
Corve Dale 46
Corwen 80
Coryton 36
Cosby 46
Costessey 40, 42
Cotham 20
Cottenham 40
Cottingham 64
Coul Point 98
Coulport 98
Coupar Angus 96
Courtmacsherry 110
Coventry 46, 49
Cover, R. 56
Coverack 14
Cowbit 40
Cowbridge 18, 82
Cowdenbeath 88
Cowes 22, 24
Cowfold 26
Cowshill 74
Coxheath 28
Coxhoe 74
Coxwold 63
Coychurch 18, 82
Craig 102
Craigandaive 98
Craigavon 110, 112
Craiglockhart 90
Craigmillar 88, 90
Craignure 100
Cramlington 74
Cramond 88, 90
Cramond I. 88
Crana 112
Cranborne Chase 18
Cranbrook 26, 28
Cranleigh 26, 30
Cranwell 54
Crawley 26, 30
Crediton 16, 18
Creech St Michael 16, 18
Cregagh 114
Cregneish 78
Crewe 46, 80
Crewkerne 18
Cribbs Causeway 20
Criccieth 80, 84
Crickhowell 82
Cricklade 18, 39
Cricklewood 34
Crigglestone 58
Crinan 98
Cringleford 40, 42
Cripp's Corner 26, 28
Croeserw 18, 82
Croftfoot 92
Crofton 58
Crofts Bank 68
Croglin 74
Cromane 118
Cromarty Firth 86
Cromer 40
Cromhall 18
Crondall 22
Crook 74
Crookham 74
Crosby 54, 66, 70
Crosby Ravensworth 72
Cross Fell 72
Crossaig 98
Crossapol Bay 100
Crosscanonby 72
Crossford 88
Crossgar 112
Crossgates 88
Crosshill 98
Crossmaglen 112
Croston 66
Crotty 82
Crouch, R. 36
Croughton 39
Crowborough 26, 28, 30
Crowland 40, 44
Crowlin Islands 102
Crowthorne 22, 30
Croy 104
Croyde 16
Croydon 30, 32
Crumlin, Dublin 116

Crumlin, N.Ireland 112
Crumlin, Wales 18, 82
Crummock Water 72
Cuckfield 26
Cuckmere, R. 26
Cuddington 70
Cuilcagh 112
Cuillin Hills 102
Cuillin Sound 102
Cul Mor 86
Cullaloe Hills 88
Cullin Hills 86
Cullin Sound 86
Cullipool 100
Cullivoe 108
Cullompton 16, 18
Cullybackey 112
Culmstock 16, 18
Culnaknock 102
Culross 88
Culswick 108
Cultra 114
Culzean Bay 98
Cumbernauld 86, 94
Cumnock 86
Cumnor 39
Cuncagh 110
Cupar 86, 96
Currie 88
Curry Rivel 18
Cushendon 110
Cwm 82
Cwmafan 18, 82
Cwmbran 18, 80, 82
Cwmllynfell 82

D
Dacre 72
Dairsie 96
Dalby 78
Dalgety Bay 88
Dalham 40
Dalkeith 88
Dalkey 116
Dalkey Island 116
Dalmally 100
Dalmeny 88
Dalry, N.Ayrshire 98
Dalry, Wales 90
Dalrymple 98
Dalston 74
Dalton 60
Dalton-in-Furness 66, 72
Damerham 18, 22
Damflask Reservoir 52
Danbury 36
Danby 63
Danderhall 88, 90
Dane, R. 46
Danehill 26
Danure 88
Darby's Bridge 118
Darenth 28
Darlington 12, 56
Darnall 60
Darndale 116
Darnley 92
Dart, R. 16
Dartford 28, 32
Dartington 16
Dartmeet 16
Dartmoor 12
Dartmoor National Park 16
Dartmouth 16
Darton 56
Darwen 66
Davaar Island 98
Daventry 46
Daviot 104
Dawlish 16, 18
Deal 28
Dean Water 96
Dearham 72
Deben, R. 40
Debenham 40
Dechmont 88
Dedham 36, 40
Deddington 39
Dee, R. 12, 46, 66, 70, 80
Deeping St Nicholas 40
Deganwy 84
Delabole 14
Delamere 70
Delph 52
Denbigh (Dinbych) 80
Denby Dale 52
Denham 32, 39
Denhead 96
Denholm 74
Denholme 58
Denmead 22
Dennington 40
Dennistoun 92
Denton 68
Denver 40, 44
Deptford 34
Derby 12, 46
Derbyhaven 78
Derg, R. 112
Derreendaragh 118
Derriana Lough 118
Derrygonnelly 112
Derrymore 118
Derryveagh Mts 110
Dersingham 40, 54
Dervaig 100
Derwent, R. 46, 56, 63
Derwent Reservoir 52, 74
Derwent Water 72
Deveron, R. 86
Devizes 18
Devon, R. 54
Dewsbury 56, 58
Dhoon 78

Dibden 22
Didcot 39
Didsbury 68
Digbeth 50
Dighty Water 96
Dinas Powys 18, 82
Dinbych (Denbigh) 80
Dingle 110, 118
Dingle Bay 110, 118
Dingwall 86, 104
Dinnington 60
Diss 40
Distington 72
Divis Mountain 114
Dobwalls 14, 16
Dochgarroch 104
Docking 40
Dodder, R. 116
Doddinghurst 36
Doddington 74
Dodman Point 14
Dogdyke 54
Dolbenmaen 84
Dolgarrog 84
Dolgellau 80
Dollis Hill 34
Don (Scotland), R. 12
Don (Yorks.), R. 60
Doncaster 56, 60
Donegal 110
Donegal Bay 12, 110, 112
Donington 40, 54
Doomanagh 118
Dorchester 18
Dordon 49
Dores 104
Dorking 30
Dornach Firth 86
Dornie 102
Dough Mountain 112
Douglas 12, 78
Doulus Head 118
Dounby 106
Doune 94
Doune Hill 94, 98
Dove, R. 40
Dove (Derbyshire), R. 46
Dove Holes 52
Dover 12, 28
Dowanhill 92
Downend 20
Downfield 96
Downham Market 40, 44
Downpatrick 110, 112
Downtown 18, 22
Dowsby 40, 54
Drayton, Norfolk 40, 42
Drayton, Oxon. 39
Drefach 82
Dreghorn 98
Drimnin 100
Drogheda 110
Dromahair 110
Dromore 110, 112
Dronfield 46, 56
Droom 118
Droylsden 68
Druidrishaig 98
Drumbeck 92
Drumchapel 92
Drumcondra 116
Drumlock Point 116
Drumnadrochit 104
Drumquin 112
Drumvaich 94
Drygarn Fawr 80
Drymen 94
Dubh Artach 98
Dublin (Baile Atha Cliath) 12, 110, 116
Dublin Bay 116
Duck End 36, 40
Duddingston 90
Duddington 88
Duddo 74
Duddon, R. 72
Dudley 46, 49
Dudley Hill 58
Duleek 110
Dullingham 40
Dulnain, R. 104
Dulverton 16, 18
Dulwich 34
Dumbarton 86, 94
Dumfries 12, 86
Dun da Ghaoithe 100
Dún Dealgan (Dundalk) 12, 110, 112
Dún Laoghaire 12, 110, 116
Dunany Point 110
Dunblane 94
Duncansby Head 86
Dundalk Bay 110, 112
Dundalk (Dún Dealgan) 12, 110, 112
Dundee 12, 86
Dundonald 114
Dundreggan 104
Dundrum Bay 110, 112
Dundrum, Dublin 116
Dundrum, N.Ireland 112
Dundry 20
Dunearn 88
Dunfermline 86, 88
Dungannon 110, 112
Dungarvan 110
Dungeness 28
Dungiven 112
Dunholme 54
Dunkery Beacon 16, 18
Dunkirk 28
Dunloy 112
Dunmanway 110
Dunmurry 112, 114
Dunnamanagh 112
Dunnet Head 86
Dunnington 56

Dunoon 98
Dunquin 118
Duns 74, 86
Dunstable 39
Dunster 16, 18
Dunvant 82
Dunvegan 102
Dunvegan Head 102
Durham 74, 86
Durrington 18, 22
Dursey Island 110
Dursley 18, 39
Dury Voe 108
Dyfi, R. 80
Dymchurch 28
Dysart 88

E
Ealing 32
Earby 66
Earith 40, 44
Earl Soham 40
Earls Colne 36, 40
Earl's Seat 94
Earlston 74
Earn, R. 96
Easdale 100
Easebourne 22, 26
Easington, Durham 74
Easington, East Riding 54, 64
Easingwold 56
East Bergholt 36, 40
East Calder 88
East Coker 18
East Compton 20
East Dean 26
East Dereham 40
East Fen 54
East Grinstead 26, 30
East Hanney 39
East Haring 40
East Horsley 30
East Hunspill 16, 18
East Keal 54
East Kilbride 86
East Looe 14, 16
East Malling 28
East Midlands Airport 46
East Preston 26
East Wittering 22, 26
East Woodhay 22
Eastbourne 26
Eastburn 56
Easter Quarff 108
Eastfield, S.Lanarks. 92
Eastfield, Yorks. 63
Eastgate 74
Eastham 70
Eastleigh 22
Easton 18, 20
Easton-in-Gordano 18, 20
Eastry 28
Eaton Bray 39
Eaton Socon 40
Ebbw Vale 80, 82
Eccles 66, 68, 74
Ecclesfield 60
Eccleston 66
Eckford 74
Eckington 39
Edale 52
Eday 106
Eden, R. 72, 74
Eden Mouth 96
Edenbridge 30
Edenderry 110
Edenfield 66
Ederny 112
Edgbaston 50
Edgbaston Reservoir 50
Edgworth 66
Edinburgh 12, 86, 88, 90
Edingham 74
Edmundbyres 74
Effingham 30, 32
Egham 30, 32
Egilsay 106
Eglingham 74
Eglinton 112
Egremont 72
Egton 63
Eigg 86
Eilean Leodhais (Isle of Lewis) 12, 86
Eilean Mor 100
Eilean Shona 100
Elgin 12, 86
Elgol 102
Elham 28
Eling 22
Ellesmere Port 46, 70, 80
Ellingham 74
Ellington 74
Elloughton 56, 64
Elm 40, 44
Elmswell 40
Elsdon 74
Elstead 22, 30
Elstree 32, 39
Elton 70
Ely, Cambs. 40, 44
Ely, Wales 18
Embleton 74
Emneth 40, 44
Emsworth 22, 26
Endrick Water 94
Enfield 32, 36, 39
Enfield, Rep. of Ireland 110
Ennerdale Water 72
Ennis (Inis) 12, 110
Enniscorthy 110
Enniskerry 110
Enniskillen 110, 112
Ennistymon 110
Enstone 39

Epping 32, 36
Epsom 30, 32
Erdington 50
Eriswell 40, 44
Erne, R. 110, 112
Erraid 100
Errigal 110, 112
Erris Head 110
Errogie 104
Errol 96
Esha Ness 108
Esher 30, 32
Esk, R. 72, 74, 86, 88
Eskbank 88, 90
Eskdale 74
Essington 49
Ettrickbridge 74
Evenlode, R. 39
Evercreech 18
Ewell 30, 32
Ewhurst 26, 30
Exe, R. 16, 18
Exebridge 16, 18
Exeter 12, 16, 18
Exminster 16, 18
Exmoor 12, 16, 18
Exmoor National Park 16, 18
Exmouth 16, 18
Eyam 52
Eye, Suffolk 40
Eye, nr P'boro 40, 44
Eyeries 118
Eynsford 28, 32
Eynsham 39
Eythorne 28

F
Fahamore 118
Failand 20
Failsworth 68
Fair Head 110
Fair Oak 22
Fairlie 98
Fairlight 26, 28
Fairmilehead 88, 90
Fakenham 40
Fal, R. 14
Falcarragh 110
Falkirk 86
Falleston 18
Falls 114
Falmouth 14
Falmouth Bay 14
Falstone 74
Fanad Head 110
Fane, R. 112
Fara 106
Fareham 22, 24
Farleigh Wallop 22
Farmborough 18
Farnborough 22, 30
Farne Islands 74
Farnham 22, 30
Farnworth 68
Farr 104
Farranfore 118
Farrar, R. 104
Farsley 58
Faslane 94
Faversham 28
Fawley 22, 244
Fazeley 49
Feale, R. 110
Fearnmore 102
Featherstone, Staffs. 49
Featherstone, Yorks. 56, 58
Feehlin, R. 104
Felixstowe 36, 40
Felling 74, 76
Felsted 36, 40
Felton 74
Feltwell 40, 44
Feniton 16, 18
Fenstanton 40
Fenwick 74
Feock 14
Feolin Ferry 98
Fermoy 110
Ferndown 18, 22
Fernhurst 22, 26
Ferns 110
Fethard 110
Fetlar 108
Ffestiniog 84
Filby Broad 42
Filey 56, 63
Fillongley 49
Filton 18, 20
Filton Airfield 20
Finaghy 114
Finchampstead 22
Finchingfield 36, 40
Findhorn, R. 104
Findon 26
Finglas 116
Finn, R. 110, 112
Finningham 40
Finningly 56
Finsbury 34
Finstown 106
Fintona 110, 112
Fintry 94
Fionn Loch 102
Fionnphort 100
Firhouse 116
Firth 108
Firth of Clyde 86, 98
Firth of Forth 86, 88, 90
Firth of Lorn 86, 100
Firth of Tay 96
Fishguard (Abergwaun) 80
Fishponds 20
Fishtoft 40, 54
Fitful Head 108

Fiunary 100
Fivemiletown 112
Fladdabister 108
Flamborough Head 56
Flat Holm 18, 82
Flax Burton 20
Fleet 22, 30
Fleetwood 66
Flempton 40
Flexbury 14, 16
Flimby 72
Flimwell 26, 28
Flint (Y Fflint) 70, 80
Flitwick 39
Flixton 68
Flodden 74
Flookburgh 72
Flotta 106
Foilclough 118
Folkestone 28
Folkingham 54
Folly Gate 14, 16
Ford, Argyll & Bute 98
Ford, Northd. 74
Fordham 40
Fordbridge 18, 22
Foreland 24
Foreland Point 16, 18
Forest of Bowland 56, 66
Forest Row 26, 30
Forkhill 112
Formby 66
Fort Augustus 104
Fort William 86, 100
Forth, R. 86, 94
Forth Bridge 88
Forth Road Bridge 88
Fortrose 104
Fortuneswell 18
Fortwilliam 114
Fotherby 54
Foulness Point 36
Foulridge 66
Fountains Abbey 56
Four Elms 30
Four Marks 22
Four Oaks 26, 28
Fowey 14
Fowey, R. 14
Foxdale 78
Foxrock 116
Foyers 104
Foyle, R. 110, 112
Foynes 110
Framfield 26
Framlingham 40
Frampton 40, 54
Frampton Cotterell 18, 20
Frampton on Severn 39
Frankley 49
Freckleton 66
Fremington 16
Frenchway 20
Frensham 22, 26, 30
Freshwater 22, 24
Frimley 22, 30
Frinton-on-Sea 36, 40
Friskney 54
Frithelstock Stone 14, 16
Frizington 72
Frodsham 70
Frogmore 22, 30
Frome 18
Frome, R. 18, 20
Fryerning 36
Fuar Bheinn 100
Fulbourn 40
Fulford 56
Fulham 32, 34
Fulwood 60
Funzie 108
Furnace 98
Fyfield 36
Fylde, R. 66

G
Gaer 82
Gailimh (Galway) 12, 110
Gainsborough 54, 56
Gair Loch 102
Gairloch 102
Gairsay 106
Gala Water 74
Galashiels 74, 86
Gallowhill 92
Galtee Mts 110
Galtymore 110
Galway Bay 12, 110
Galway (Gailimh) 12, 110
Gamlingay 40
Garabal 94
Garahban Forest 94
Garderhouse 108
Gare Loch 94, 98
Garelochhead 98
Garforth 58
Gargrave 66
Gargunnock Hills 94
Garmony 100
Garstang 66
Garston 70
Gartachoil 94
Gartocham 94
Garton 64
Garvagh 112
Garvard 98
Garvellachs 94
Gateshead 74, 76
Gatley 68
Gatwick 26, 30
Gawthrop 72
Gayton 40
Gedney Drove End 40, 54
Gelligaer 18, 82

Georgeham 16
Gerrards Cross 32, 39
Giant's Causeway 110, 112
Gibraltar Point 54
Giffnock 92
Gigha 98
Gilford 112
Gillamoor 63
Gillingham, Dorset 18
Gillingham, Kent 28
Gilsland 74
Gilwern 82
Girlsta 108
Girton 40
Glamorgan 82
Glan Conwy 84
Glanaman 82
Glanaruddery Mts 118
Glanmore Lake 118
Glanton 74
Glasgow 12, 86
Glastonbury 18
Gleadless 60
Glemsford 36, 40
Glen Affric 104
Glen Artnmey 94
Glen Cannich 104
Glen Coe 100
Glen Finglas Reservoir 94
Glen More 86, 104
Glen Moriston 104
Glen Nevis 100
Glen Shiel 102
Glen Vine 78
Glenacardoch Point 98
Glenariff 112
Glenarm 112
Glenbar 98
Glenbeg 100
Glenbeg Lough 118
Glenbeigh 118
Glenbrittle 102
Glencairn 114
Glencarse 96
Glencoe 100
Glendaruel 98
Glendun 112
Glenegedale 98
Glenelg 102
Glengarriff 118
Glengyle 94
Glenrothes 86
Glenties 110
Glenveagh National Park 110
Gletness 108
Glinton 40
Glossop 52, 56
Gloucester 12, 39
Glusburn 56
Glyder Fawr 84
Glyn-Neath 82
Glyncorrwg 18, 82
Gneevgullia 118
Goat Fell 98
Goathland 63
Godalming 30
Godmanchester 40
Godstone 30, 32
Goldcliff 18
Golden Pot 22, 26
Goldthorpe 60
Gometra 100
Goodie Water 94
Goole 56
Goonhaven 14
Gordon 74
Gorey 110
Goring 22
Gorseinon 82
Gorton 82
Gorumna Island 110
Gosberton 40, 54
Gosfield 36, 40
Gosforth, Cumbria 72
Gosforth, Tyne and Wear 74, 76
Gosport 22, 24
Goudhurst 26, 28
Govan 92
Govanhill 92
Gowy, R. 70
Goxhill 54, 64
Goyt, R. 68
Graemsay 106
Grafham Water 40
Graiguenamanagh 110
Grain 28
Grampian Mts 12, 86
Grampound 14
Granard 110
Grand Canal 110, 116
Grange 96
Grange-over-Sands 66, 72
Grangetown 18, 82
Grantham 46, 54
Granton 90
Grasmere 72
Gravelly Hill 50
Gravesend 28
Grayrigg 72
Grays 28, 36
Grayshott 22, 26, 30
Greasbrough 60
Greasby 70
Great Ayton 56, 63
Great Baddow 36
Great Barton 40
Great Bentley 36, 40
Great Bircham 40
Great Blasket Island 118
Great Boughton 63
Great Clifton 72
Great Cornard 36, 40
Great Cymbrae 98

Great Dodd 72
Great Driffield 56
Great Dunmow 36, 40
Great Eccleston 66
Great Ellingham 40
Great Gonerby 54
Great Gransden 40
Great Harwood 66
Great Horkesley 36, 40
Great Malvern 46
Great Marton 66
Great Missenden 39
Great Ormes Head 80, 84
Great Ouse, R. 40, 44, 46
Great Ponton 54
Great Salkeld 72, 74
Great Sampford 36, 40
Great Shelford 40
Great Stour, R. 28
Great Torrington 14, 16
Great Wakering 36
Great Waltham 36, 40
Great Whernside 56
Great Yarmouth 40, 42
Great Yeldham 36, 40
Greater Manchester 56, 66
Greatham 22, 26
Greatstone-on-Sea 28
Green Park 34
Greenham 22
Greenhead 74
Greenigo 106
Greenisland 112
Greenlaw 74
Greenock 86, 94, 98
Greenodd 72
Greenore 110
Greenwich 32, 34
Greenwich Park 34
Greta, R. 56, 66, 72
Gretna 74
Greystoke 72
Greystones 110
Grimoldby 54
Grimsby 12, 54, 56, 64
Grimston 40
Gritley 106
Grizebeck 72
Grosmoor 63
Grove 39
Grutness 108
Guardbridge 96
Guide Post 74
Guildford 30
Guildtown 96
Guisborough 56, 63
Guiseley 56, 58
Gunna 100
Gunningsburgh 108
Gunnislake 14, 16
Gurnos 82
Gust 40
Gutcher 108
Gwaun-Cae-Gurwen 82
Gweebarra Bay 110, 112
Gweedore 110, 112
Gwithian 14
Gwytherin 84

H
Hacking Broad 40
Hacklinge 28
Hackness 63
Haddenham, Bucks. 39
Haddenham, Cambs. 40, 44
Haddington 86
Haddiscoe 40, 42
Hadleigh 36, 40
Hadrian's Wall 74
Hagley 49
Hag's Head 110
Hailsham 26
Halbeath 88
Halberton 16, 18
Hale 40, 42
Hales 40, 42
Halesowen 46, 49
Halesworth 40
Halewood 70
Halifax 56, 58
Halland 26
Hallen 20
Hallworthy 14, 16
Halsham 64
Halstead 36, 40
Halton, Bucks. 39
Halton, Lancs. 66, 70
Haltwhistle 74
Halwell 16
Hamble-le-Rice 22
Hambleton 66
Hamilton 86
Hammersmith 34
Hamnavoe, Burra 108
Hamnavoe, Shetland 108
Hamnavoe, Yell 108
Hampreston 18
Hampshire Downs 22
Hampstead 32, 34
Hamstead 50
Hamstreet 26, 28
Handsworth, B'ham 50
Handsworth, Yorks. 60
Hanham 18, 20
Happisburgh 40
Harbledown 28
Harborne 50
Hare Street 36, 40
Harefield 32, 39
Harehills 58
Harewood 56
Harlech 84
Harlesden 34
Harleston 40

Harlington 39
Harlow 36, 40
Haroldswick 108
Harpendon 39, 40
Harpurhey 68
Harrietsham 28
Harrogate 56
Harston 40
Harter Falls 72
Hartfield 26
Hartland 16
Hartland Point 16
Hartlepool 74, 86
Hartley, Kent 28
Hartley, Northumberland 76
Hartley Wintney 22
Harton 76
Hartshill 49
Harwell 39
Harwich 36, 40
Harworth 60
Hascosay 108
Haslemere 22, 26, 30
Haslingden 66
Hastings 26
Hatfield 39
Hatfield Broad Oak 36, 40
Hatfield Peverel 36
Hatfield, S.Yorks. 56
Hatherleigh 14, 16
Hathersage 52, 60
Hathershaw 68
Havant 22, 24, 26
Haverfordwest 12, 80
Haverhill 36, 40
Hawarden 70
Haweswater Reservoir 72
Hawick 74, 86
Hawkesbury 18, 39
Hawkhead 92
Hawkhurst 26, 28
Hawkinge 28
Hawkshead 72
Hawkwell 36
Hawley 22, 30
Hawnby 63
Haworth 56
Haxey 56
Haydock 66, 70
Haydon Bridge 74
Haydon Wick 18, 39
Hayfield 52
Hayle 14
Hayling Island 22, 26
Hayton 74
Haywards Heath 26
Hazel Grove 52
Hazelwood 114
Hazlemere 39
Heacham 40, 54
Headcom 28
Headley 22, 26, 30
Heads of Ayr 98
Healabhal Bheag 102
Healing 54, 56, 64
Heanor 46
Heanton Punchardon 16
Heathfield 26, 28
Heathrow 30, 32
Heaton 76
Heaton Moor 68
Heaviley 68
Hebburn 76
Heckington 40, 54
Heckmondwike 58
Hedge End 22
Hedon 64
Heeley 60
Heighington 54
Helensburgh 94, 98
Helhoughton 40
Hellingly 26
Helmsdale, R. 86
Helmsley 63
Helpringham 54
Helsby 70
Helston 14
Helvellyn 72
Hemel Hempstead 39
Hemmingford Grey 40
Hempnall 40, 42
Hempstead 36, 40
Hemsby 40, 42
Hemyock 16, 18
Hendon, Greater London 32, 39
Hendon, Tyne and Wear 76
Henfield 26
Hengoed 18, 82
Hengrove 20
Henley-on-Thames 22
Henlow 39, 40
Henstridge 18
Herbury 20
Hereford 46, 80
Heriot 74
Herma Ness 108
Herne Bay 28
Herstmonceux 26
Herston 106
Hertford 39, 40
Heswall 70
Hethersett 40, 42
Hetton 56, 66
Hetton-le-Hole 74
Hexham 74
Hextable 28, 30, 32
Heybridge 36
Hibaldstow 54, 64
Hickling Broad 42
High Bentham 66
High Garrett 36, 40
High Green 60
High Halden 26, 28
High Hawsker 63

High Hesket 74
High Legh 66
High Lorton 72
High Peak 52, 56
High Seat 56
High Wycombe 39
Higham 28
Highampton 14, 16
Highbridge 16, 18
Highbury 34
Highclere 22
Higher Blackley 68
Highgate 50
Highnam 39
Hightown 70
Highworth 18, 39
Hildenborough 28
Hilgay 40, 44
Hill of Stake 98
Hill Top 68
Hillend 88
Hillington 92
Hillside 108
Hillswick 108
Hilperton 18
Hilpsford Point 66
Hinckley 46
Hinderwell 63
Hindhead 22, 26, 30
Hindley 66, 70
Hindon 18
Hingham 40
Hipperholme 58
Hirwaun 82
Histon 40
Hitchin 39, 40
Hither Green 34
Hobson 76
Hockley 36
Hoddesdon 36
Hodgehill 50
Hogsthorpe 54
Holbeach 40, 54
Holbeach Marsh 40, 54
Holborn 34
Holbrook 36, 40
Holderness 64
Holkyn 70
Holland Fen 40, 54
Holland-on-Sea 36, 40
Hollandstoun 106
Hollesley Bay 36, 40
Hollington 26
Hollingworth 52
Holme-on-Spalding-Moor 56
Holmesfield 52
Holmfirth 52, 56
Holsworthy 14, 16
Holt 18
Holt, Norfolk 40
Holton le Clay 64
Holy Island (Lindisfarne) 74
Holy Island, Scotland 98
Holy Island, Wales 80
Holyhead (Caergybi) 80
Holywell 70
Holywood 114
Holywood Hills 114
Homersfield 40
Honiton 16, 18
Hoo 28
Hook 22
Hook Island 110
Hook Norton 39
Hopton, Norfolk 40, 42
Hopton, Suffolk 40
Horam 26, 28
Horbling 40, 54
Hordle 22, 24
Horley 30
Hornby 72
Horncastle 54
Horndead 22
Hornfield 20
Horning 40, 42
Hornsea 56
Hornsea Mere 42
Horrabridge 14, 16
Horringer 40
Horsford 40, 42
Horsforth 58
Horsham 26, 30
Horsmonden 26, 28
Horstead 40, 42
Horton Heath 22
Horwich 66
Hotwells 20
Houbie 108
Houghton 74
Houghton le Spring 74, 76
Houghton Regis 39
Houndslow 74
Housesteads 74
Houston 98
Houton 106
Hoveton 40, 42
Howardian Hills 56
Howden 56
Howden Reservoir 52
Howth 116
Hoy 86, 106
Hoylake 70
Hoyland 60
Hucknall 46
Huddersfield 56, 58
Huish Episcopi 18
Hullavington 18
Hullbridge 36
Humber 12
Humber Bridge 64
Humberside Airport 54, 56, 64
Humberston 54, 64
Humbleton Hills 63
Humshaugh 74

Hundleby 54
Hungerford 22
Hunmanby 56, 63
Hunstanton 40, 54
Hunter's Quay 98
Huntingdon 40, 44
Hursley 22
Hurst Green 26, 28
Hurstbourne Tarrant 22
Hurstpierpoint 26
Huttoft 54
Hutton 18
Hutton Rudby 63
Huyton 66, 70
Hyde 52, 56, 66
Hyde Park 34
Hynish 100
Hynish Bay 100
Hythe 28
Hythe (Hants) 22, 24

I
Ibrox 92
Icklesham 26, 28
Icklingham 40
Idle, R. 56
Idmiston 22
Idrigil 102
Ilchester 18
Ilem, R. 110
Ilford 32, 36
Ilfracombe 16
Ilkeston 46
Ilkley 56
Ilminster 18
Islington 16, 18
Immingham 54, 56, 64
Immingham Dock 64
Impington 40
Inch, Edinburgh 90
Inch Gavie 88
Inch, Kerry 118
Inchcolm 88
Inchkeith 88
Inchmickery 88
Inchture 96
Ingatestone 36
Ingleborough 56, 66
Ingleton 66, 72
Inglewood Forest 72
Ingoldmells 54
Inis (Ennis) 12, 110
Inishark 110
Inishbofin 110
Inisheer 110
Inishman 110
Inishmore 110
Inishowen 110, 112
Inishowen Head 110
Inishtooskert 118
Inishtrahull 110
Inishturk 110
Inishvickillane 118
Innellan 98
Inner Sound 86, 102
Innerleithen 74
Inny 118
Inny, R. 110
Inveralligin 102
Inveraray 100
Inverarity 96
Inverarnan 94
Inverbeg 94
Invercharnan 100
Inveresk 88
Inverinan 100
Inverkeithing 88
Inverleith 90
Invermoriston 104
Inverness 86, 104
Invernoaden 98
Inversnaid 94
Inveruglas 94
Inverurie 86
Iona 86, 100
Iona Abbey 100
Ipplepen 16, 18
Ipswich 12, 36, 40
Ireland's Eye 116
Irishmurray 110
Irthing, R. 74
Irton Acton 20
Irvine 86, 98
Irvine Bay 98
Irwell, R. 68
Isbister 108
Isbister, Mainland 108
Isbister, Whalsay 108
Isla, R. 96
Island Magee 110, 112
Islay 12, 86, 98
Isle of Angelsey 84
Isle of Dogs 34
Isle of Ely 40, 44
Isle of Grain 28
Isle of Lewis (Eilean Leodhais) 12, 86
Isle of Man 12, 78
Isle of Man Airport 78
Isle of Noss 108
Isle of Portland 18
Isle of Purbeck 18
Isle of Sheppey 28
Isle of Thanet 28
Isle of Walney 66
Isle of Wight 12, 22, 24
Iseham 40, 44
Isles of Scilly 12
Islington 32, 34
Istead Rise 28
Iver 32
Iveragh 118

Ivinghoe 39
Iwade 28
Ixworth 40

J
Jarrow 74, 76
Jaywick 36, 40
Jedburgh 74
Jesmond 76
Jura 12, 86, 98

K
Kaimes 88, 90
Kale Water 74
Kames 98
Kanturk 110
Keady 112
Kealkill 118
Kearsley 68
Kedington 36, 40
Keelby 54, 64
Keighley 56, 58
Keilmore 98
Kellas 96
Kells, Kerry 118
Kells, Meath 110
Kells, N. Ireland 112
Kells, R. 112
Kelsall 70
Kelso 74
Kelty 88
Kelvedon 36, 40
Kelvedon Hatch 32, 36
Kelvindale 92
Kelvingrove 92
Kelvinside 92
Kendal 72
Kenfig 18, 82
Kenmare 110, 118
Kenmare River 110, 118
Kennacraig 98
Kennet, R. 22
Kennington 34
Kennington, Oxon. 39
Kensaleyre 102
Kensington 34
Kensworth 39
Kent, R. 72
Kentallen 100
Kenton 16, 18
Kerrera 100
Kerry Head 110
Kershopefoot 74
Kesgrave 36, 40
Kesh 112
Kessingland 40
Keswick 72
Kettering 46
Kettletoft 106
Kewstoke 18
Keyingham 54, 64
Keymer 26
Keynsham 18, 20
Kidderminster 46
Kidlington 39
Kidsgrove 46
Kidwelly 82
Kielder Water 74
Kilarney 12
Kilbarrack 116
Kilberry 98
Kilbirnie 98
Kilbrannan Sound 98
Kilbride 100
Kilburn 34
Kilchenzie 98
Kilchoan 100
Kilchrenan 100
Kilcock 110
Kilcreggan 98
Kilcummin 118
Kildare 110
Kildonan 98
Kilfinan 98
Kilflynn 118
Kilgarvan 118
Kilgobnet 118
Kilham 74
Kilkee 110
Kilkeel 112
Kilkenny (Cill Chainnigh) 12, 110
Kilkhampton 14, 16
Kilkinlea 118
Killabunane 118
Killala 110
Killala Bay 110
Killaloe 110
Killarney (Cill Airne) 110, 118
Killarney National Park 110, 118
Killary Harbour 110
Killean 98
Killearn 94
Killiney 116
Killiney Bay 116
Killingworth 74, 76
Killorglin 110, 118
Killundine 100
Killybegs 110
Kilmacolm 98
Kilmalieu 100
Kilmaluag 102
Kilmany 96
Kilmarnock 12, 86
Kilmartin 98
Kilmelford 100
Kilmington 16, 18
Kilmory 98, 102
Kilninian 100
Kilninver 100
Kilnsea 64
Kilnsea Clays 64
Kiloran 98
Kiloran Bay 98
Kilrush 110

Kilsyth 94
Kilwinning 98
Kimberley 40
Kimpton 39, 40
Kinder Scout 52
Kineton 39
Kingarth 98
Kinghorn 88
Kingkerswell 16
Kings Langley 32, 39
King's Lynn 40
King's Park 92
King's Sutton 39
King's Worthy 22
Kingsbridge 16
Kingsbury 49
Kingsbury Episcopi 18
Kingsclere 22
Kingscourt 110
Kingsdown 28
Kingseat 88
Kingskerswell 16, 18
Kingsnorth 26, 28
Kingsteignton 16, 18
Kingston Seymour 18
Kingston upon Hull 12, 54, 56, 64
Kingston upon Thames 30, 32
Kingswear 16
Kingswood 18, 20
Kingswood, Surrey 30, 32
Kingussie 86
Kinloch 102
Kinloch Hourn 102
Kinlochard 94
Kinlochewe 102
Kinlochleven 100
Kinnegad 110
Kinsale 110
Kintbury 22
Kintour 98
Kintyre 86, 98, 110
Kippax 58
Kippen 94
Kirbymoorside 56, 63
Kircudbright 86
Kirk Michael 78
Kirk Yetholm 74
Kirkby 66, 70
Kirkby Lonsdale 66, 72
Kirkby Thore 72
Kirkcaldy 86, 88
Kirkham 66
Kirkheaton 58
Kirklevington 63
Kirkliston 88
Kirknewton 74
Kirkoswald 74
Kirkoswald, S.Ayrshire 98
Kirkstall 58
Kirkton 98
Kirkton of Lethendry 96
Kirkwall 12, 106
Kirtlington 39
Kirton, Essex 36
Kirton, Lincs. 40, 54
Kirton in Lindsey 54, 56
Knapdale 98
Knaresborough 56
Knayton 63
Knebworth 39, 40
Knighton 80
Knightstown 118
Knock, Belfast 114
Knock, Mull 100
Knockaboy 110, 118
Knockalong 110
Knockanefune 118
Knockmealdown Mts 110
Knocknadober 118
Knocknagashel 118
Knocknagoney 114
Knocknagree 118
Knocknagullion 118
Knocksharry 78
Knowle, N.Somerset 20
Knowle, W.Midlands 49
Knoydart 102
Knutsford 56
Kyle of Lochalsh 102
Kyleakin 102
Kylerhea 102
Kyles of Bute 98

L
Laceby 54, 64
Lacock 18
Ladhar Bheinn 102
Lady Isle 98
Ladybower Reservoir 46, 52
Ladybrook 114
Ladykirk 74
Ladywood 50
Lagan, R. 112, 114
Laganulva 100
Lake District National Park 72
Lake of Menteith 94
Lakenheath 40, 44
Laleston 82
Lambay Island 110
Lamberhurst 26, 28
Lambeth 34
Lambourn 22
Lambourn Downs 22
Lamb's Head 118
Lamesley 74, 76
Lamlash 98
Lampeter 80
Lanark 86
Lancashire Plain 66
Lancaster 66
Lancaster Canal 66
Lanchester 74
Landguard Point 36, 40

Landore 82
Land's End 12, 14
Lane End 39
Langford 40
Langholm 74
Langley Green 50
Langsett Reservoir 52
Langside 92
Langstrothdale Chase 66
Langwathby 72
Lanivet 14
Lanport 18
Lapford 16, 18
Largs 98
Larkhill 18, 22
Larling 40
Larne 10, 112
Latchingdon 36
Lauder 74
Lauder Water 74
Launceston 14, 16
Laune, R. 118
Lauragh 118
Lavenham 40
Lavernock Point 18, 82
Lawford 36, 40
Laxey 78
Laxey Bay 78
Laxo 108
Layer de la Haye 40
Lazonby 74
Leadenham 54
Leadgate 74, 76
Leasingham 54
Leatherhead 30, 32
Lechlade 18, 39
Ledaig 100
Ledburn 39
Ledbury 80
Lee, R. 110
Lee-on-Solent 22
Leeds 12, 6, 58
Leeds-Bradford Airport 56, 58
Leedstown 14
Leek 46
Leeming 56
Leenane 110
Legoniel 114
Leicester 12, 46
Leigh 66, 70
Leigh Woods 20
Leighlinbridge 110
Leighton Buzzard 39
Leiston 40
Leith 88, 90
Leith Hill 26, 30
Lenham 28
Lennoxtown 94
Leominster 46, 80
Lerrig 118
Lerwick 108
Lesbury 74
Letchworth 39, 40
Letheringsett 40
Letterfinlin 118
Letterkenny 110, 112
Leuchars 96
Levens 72
Levenshulme 68
Levenwick 108
Lewes 26
Lewisham 34
Leyland 66
Leysdown-on-Sea 28
Leyton 34
Liathach 86, 102
Liddel, R. 74
Liddesdale 74
Liffey, R. 110, 116
Lifford 110, 112
Lifton 14, 16
Lightwater 30
Lilliesleaf 74
Limavady 110, 112
Limekilns 88
Limerick (Luimneach) 12, 110
Lincoln 12, 46, 54
Lincolnshire Wolds 56
Lindfield 26
Lindisfarne 74
Lindley 56
Lindores 96
Linford 36
Ling, R. 102
Lingfield 30
Lingwood 40, 42
Linksness 106
Linktown 88
Linlithgow 88
Linton 36, 40
Liphook 22, 26, 30
Lisbellaw 112
Lisburn 110, 112
Liscannor Bay 110
Lisdoonvarna 110
Liskeard 14, 16
Lismore, Firth of Lorn 100
Lismore, Rep. of Ireland 110
Lisnaskea 112
Lispole 118
Liss 26
Lissatinning Bridge 118
Listowel 110
Listry 118
Liswerry 18
Litherland 70
Little Bromwich 50
Little Clacton 40
Little Colonsay 100
Little Common 26
Little Cumbrae 98
Little Dart, R. 16, 18

Little Downham 40
Little Minch 86
Little Missenden 39
Little Oakley 36, 40
Little Ouse, R. 40, 44
Little Paxton 40
Littlehampton 26
Littlemore 39
Littleport 40, 44
Littlestone-on-Sea 28
Littleton 22
Liverpool 12, 46, 66, 70, 80
Liverpool Bay 66, 70
Liversedge 58
Livingston 86, 88
Lizard 14
Lizard Point 12, 14
Llanaelhaearn 84
Llanarthney 82
Llanberis 84
Llanddarog 82
Llanddeiniolen 84
Llandderfel 84
Llandeilo 80, 82
Llandovery 80
Llandrindod Wells 80
Llandudno 80, 84
Llandwrog 84
Llandybie 82
Llanegwad 82
Llanelli 80, 82
Llanelly 82
Llanerchymedd 82
Llanfair Talhaiarn 84
Llanfairfechan 84
Llanfairpwllgwyngyll 84
Llangefni 80, 84
Llangernyw 84
Llangoed 84
Llangollen 80
Llangristiolus 84
Llangurig 80
Llangynidr 82
Llanharan 18, 82
Llanidloes 80
Llanishen 18, 82
Llanllyfni 84
Llannon 82
Llannor 84
Llanrhiddian 82
Llanrhidian 82
Llanrug 84
Llanrumney 18, 82
Llanrwst 84
Llansanffraid 84
Llansannan 84
Llantrisant 18, 82
Llantwit 18
Llantwit Major 82
Llanuwchllyn 84
Llanwnda 84
Llanystumdwy 84
Lleyn Peninsula 84
Llyn Alaw 84
Llyn Brenig 84
Llyn Celyn 84
Llyn Cowlyd Reservoir 84
Llyn Tegid (Bala Lake) 80, 84
Llyn Trawsfynydd 84
Loanhead 88
Loans 98
Loch Achray 94
Loch Alsh 102
Loch Ard 94
Loch Ard Forest 94
Loch Arienas 100
Loch Ashie 104
Loch Avich 100
Loch Awe 86, 100
Loch Ba 100
Loch Bracaddale 102
Loch Brittle 102
Loch Buie 100
Loch Carron 102
Loch Cluanie 104
Loch Coalisport 98
Loch Creran 100
Loch Damh 102
Loch Duich 102
Loch Duntelchaig 104
Loch Dunvegan 102
Loch Eatharna 100
Loch Eck 98
Loch Eil 100
Loch Eishort 102
Loch Etive 100
Loch Frisa 100
Loch Fyne 86, 98
Loch Goil 98
Loch Gorm 98
Loch Gruinart 98
Loch of Harray 106
Loch Hourn 102
Loch Indaal 98
Loch Katrine 94
Loch Kishorn 102
Loch Leven 100
Loch Linnhe 100
Loch Lomond 94, 98
Loch Long 94, 98, 102
Loch Lubnaig 94
Loch Maree 102
Loch Melfort 100
Loch Mhor 104
Loch Monar 104
Loch Mullardoch 104
Loch na Keal 100
Loch na Sealga 102
Loch Nant 100
Loch Ness 12, 104
Loch Nevis 102
Loch Quoich 102
Loch Right Mor 98
Loch Scavaig 102

Loch Scridain 100
Loch Shiel 100
Loch Snizort 102
Loch Spelve 100
Loch Staosnaig 98
Loch of Stenness 106
Loch Strwen 98
Loch Sunart 100
Loch Sween 98
Loch Tarbert 98
Loch Torridon 102
Loch Tuath 100
Loch Voil 94
Lochaber 100
Lochaline 100
Lochawe 100
Lochbuie 100
Lochcarron 102
Lochdon 100
Lochee 96
Lochgelly 88
Lochgilphead 98
Lochgoilhead 98
Lochond 104
Lochranza 98
Lochwinnoch 98
Lock Venachar 94
Locking 18
Lockton 63
Loddiswell 16
Loddon 40, 42
Loftus 56, 63
Loghrea 110
London 12, 30, 32, 34, 36, 39
London City Airport 32, 36
London Colney 39
Londonderry 12, 86, 110, 112
Long Ashton 18, 20
Long Bennington 54
Long Compton 39
Long Crendon 39
Long Eaton 46
Long Hanborough 39
Long Hermiston 90
Long Melford 36, 40
Long Stratton 40, 42
Long Sutton 18
Long Sutton, The Wash 40
Longbenton 74, 76
Longbridge Deverill 18
Longford 110
Longforgan 96
Longframlington 74
Longhope 106
Longhorsley 74
Longhouton 74
Longridge 66
Longships 14
Longstone 90
Longton 66
Longtown 74
Longwell Green 20
Loop Head 110
Loose 28
Lopcombe Corner 18, 22
Lostwithiel 14
Loth 106
Lough 12
Lough Allen 110, 112
Lough Arrow 110, 112
Lough Caragh 118
Lough Con 110
Lough Corrib 110
Lough Currane 118
Lough Derg 110, 112
Lough Erne 110, 112
Lough Foyle 110, 112
Lough Gara 110, 112
Lough Gill 112
Lough Guitane 118
Lough Key 112
Lough Leane 118
Lough Mask 110
Lough Melvin 110
Lough Neagh 110, 112
Lough Oughter 112
Lough Ree 110
Lough Sheelin 110
Lough Swilly 110, 112
Loughborough 46
Lougher 118
Lougher, R. 82
Loughlinstown 116
Loughor 82
Loughros More Bay 112
Loughton 32, 36
Louth 54, 56
Low Street 40, 42
Lower Beeding 26
Lower Diabaig 102
Lower Kilchattan 98
Lower Killeyan 98
Lower Lough Erne 110, 112
Lowestoft 40, 42
Lowick 74
Loxley, R. 60
Lozells 50
Ludgershall 22
Ludgvan 14
Ludlow 46, 80
Lugg, R. 46, 80
Luib 102
Luimneach (Limerick) 12, 110
Luing 100
Lune, R. 72
Lungnaquilla Mts 110
Lunna Ness 108
Lurgan 110, 112
Luss 94, 98
Lussa Loch 98
Lusta 102
Luton 12, 39, 40
Luxulyan 14

Lydd 28
Lydford 14, 16
Lyme Bay 18
Lyme Regis 16, 18
Lyminge 28
Lymington 22, 24
Lymm 66, 70
Lympne 28
Lympstone 16, 18
Lyndhurst 22
Lyne, R. 74
Lynemouth 74
Lyness 106
Lynher, R. 14, 16
Lynmouth 16, 18
Lynton 16, 18
Lytchett 18
Lytchett Minster 18
Lytham St Anne's 66

M
Mablethorpe 54
Macclesfield 46, 52
Macgillycuddy's Reeks 110, 118
Machen 18, 82
Machir Bay 98
Machrihanish 98
Machynlleth 80
Macroom 110
Madron 14
Maentwrog 84
Maesteg 18, 80, 82
Maghanlawaun 118
Maghera 110, 112
Magherafelt 110, 112
Maghull 70
Maiden Bradley 18
Maiden Newton 18
Maidenhead 22
Maidens 98
Maidstone 28
Main, R. 112
Mainland, Orkney 86, 106
Mainland, Shetland 12, 86
Malcolm's Point 100
Maldon 36
Malin 110
Malin Head 12, 110, 112
Mallaig 86, 102
Mallow 110
Malltraeth Bay 84
Malmesbury 18, 39
Malone 114
Malpas 18, 82
Maltby 56, 60
Maltby le Marsh 54
Malton 56
Malvern Hills 46
Manby 54
Mancetter 49
Manchester 12, 56, 66
Manchester Ship Canal 68, 70
Manea 40, 44
Mangerton Mountain 118
Mangotsfield 18, 20
Manningtree 36, 40
Mansewood 92
Mansfield 46
Manston 18
Marazion 14
March 40, 44
Marden 28
Marefield 26
Mareham le Fen 54
Margam 18, 82
Margate 28
Margery Hill 52
Marham 40, 44
Marino 116
Mark 16, 18
Market Deeping 40
Market Harborough 46
Market Lavington 18
Market Rasen 54, 56
Market Weighton 56
Marks Tey 36, 40
Markyate 39
Marlborough 18, 22
Marlborough Downs 18, 22
Marldon 16
Marlow 39
Marnhull 18
Marple 52
Marsden 76
Marshfield 18
Marston 39
Marston Magna 18
Martham 40, 42
Martlesham 36, 40
Martock 18
Marybank 104
Maryfield 108
Maryhill 92
Maryport 72
Mastergeehy 118
Matlock 46
Matravers Upton 18
Mattishall 40
Maughold 78
Maughold Head 78
Mauldon 39
Mavis Grind 108
Mawnan 14
May 104
May, R. 110, 112
Maybole 98
Mayfield 26, 28
Maynooth 110
Meadowhall 60
Meal Fuar-mhonaidh 104
Meall Buidhe 102
Meare 18
Mease, R. 46

Medstead 22
Medway 28
Medway, R. 28
Meigle 96
Meikle Bin 94
Meikle Kilmory 98
Meikleour 96
Melbourn 36, 40
Melby 108
Melksham 18
Mellte, R. 82
Melmerby 72, 74
Melrose 74
Melton 40
Melton Mowbray 46
Menai Bridge 84
Menai Strait 84
Mendip Hills 18
Menheniot 14, 16
Menston 58
Merchiston 90
Mere 18
Meriden 49
Merrick 86
Merriott 18
Merry Hill 50
Mersea Island 36
Mersey, R. 46, 66, 68
Merseyside 66, 70
Merthyr Tydfil 80, 82
Messingham 54, 64
Metfield 40
Metheringham 54
Methwold 40, 44
Mevagissey 14
Mexborough 56, 60
Mhic Fhearchair 102
Mid Yell 108
Midbea 106
Mid-Calder 88
Middle Barton 39
Middle Rasen 54
Middlemarsh 18
Middlesbrough 12, 56, 63
Middleton 40
Middleton, Lancs. 66, 68
Middleton Stoney 39
Middleton, W. Yorks. 58
Middleton-on-Sea 26
Midhurst 22, 26
Midleton 110
Midleton 110
Midsomer Norton 18
Milborne Port 18
Milborne St Andrew 18
Mildenhall 40, 44
Mile End 36, 40
Milfield 74
Milford 26, 30
Milford Haven 80
Milford-on-Sea 22, 24
Millbrook 14, 16
Millisle 112
Millom 66, 72
Milltown, Dingle 118
Milltown, Kerry 118
Milngavie 94
Milnthorpe 66, 72
Milovaig 102
Milton Abbot 14, 16
Milton Keynes 12, 39, 46
Milton, Loch Ness 104
Milton, Stirling 94
Milton, Tayside 96
Milverton 16, 18
Minard 98
Minch Moor 74
Mine Head 110
Minehead 16, 18
Minster 28
Mirfield 58
Mitchelstown 110
Mizen Head 110
Moate 110
Modbury 16
Moel Sych 80
Moelfre 82
Moidart 100
Mold 46
Mole, R. 16, 18
Monadhliath Mts 86, 104
Monaghan 12, 110, 112
Moneymore 112
Monifieth 96
Monimail 96
Monks Leigh 36, 40
Monkseaton 76
Monkstown 116
Monkton 76
Monmouth (Trefynwy) 80
Montogmery (Trefaldwyn) 80
Monton 68
Montpelier 20
Moorside 68
Morar 102
Moray Firth 12, 104
Morebattle 74
Morecambe Bay 66, 72
Moredun 90
Moresby 72
Moreton-in-Marsh 39
Moretonhampstead 16, 18
Moriston, R. 104
Morley 58
Morningside 88, 90
Morpeth 74
Morriston 82
Morte Bay 16
Mortehoe 16
Mortimer 22
Mortlake 34
Morton 40, 54
Morvern 86, 100
Morwenstow 14, 16

Mosborough 56, 60
Moseley 50
Moss Side 68
Mossley Hall 70
Mosspark 92
Motherwell 86
Moulsecoomb 26
Moulton 40, 54
Mouncollins 118
Mount Bellew 110
Mount Gilbert 114
Mount Leinster 110
Mountain Ash 82
Mountmellick 110
Mount's Bay 14
Mourne Mountains 110, 112
Mousa 108
Mouth of the Humber 54, 56, 64
Mouth of the Shannon 110
Moyer 112
Moygashel 112
Muck 98
Muckle Flugga 108
Muckle Roe 108
Muckross 118
Muine 110
Muir of Ord 104
Muirdrum 96
Muirhead 96
Mulbarton 40, 42
Mulhaddart 116
Mull 12, 86, 100
Mull Head, Mainland 106
Mull Head, Papa Westray 106
Mull of Kintyre 86, 98, 110
Mull of Oa 98
Mullach Coire 102
Mullaghmore 112
Mullingar 12, 110
Mullion 14
Mumbles Head 82
Mundersley 40
Mundford 40
Munlochy 104
Murrayfield 90
Musbury 18
Musselburgh 88
Mutton Island 110
Mweelrea Mts 110
Mylor 14
Mynydd Eppynt 80
Mynydd Hiraethog 84
Mynydd Preseli 80

N
Naas (An Nás) 110
Nadder, R. 18, 22
Nailsea 18
Nairn 86, 104
Nairn, R. 104
Nantwich 80
Narbeth 80
Narborough 40
Navan (An Uaimh) 110
Nave Island 98
Nazeing 36
Neagh 12
Near Sawrey 72
Neath 18, 80, 82
Neath, R. 82
Necton 40
Needham Market 40
Needingworth 40
Nelson 56, 66
Nenagh 110
Nene, R. 40, 44, 46
Nenthead 74
Nephin 110
Nephin Beg Range 110
Ness, R. 104
Neston 80
Nether Stowey 16, 18
Netherton 74
Nettleham 54
New Addington 30, 32
New Alresford 22
New Ash Green 28
New Brighton 70
New Mills 52
New Milton 18, 22
New Mistley 36, 40
New Moston 68
New Polzeath 14
New Quay 80
New Romeny 28
New Ross 110
New Scone 96
New Town 90
New Tredegar 82
New Waltham 54, 64
Newark-on-Trent 46, 54
Newbiggin-by-the-Sea 74
Newbridge, Scotland 82, 88
Newbridge, Wales 18, 82
Newburgh 96
Newburn 76
Newbury 22
Newby Bridge 72
Newcastle 110, 112
Newcastle Emlyn 80
Newcastle upon Tyne 12, 74, 76, 86
Newcastle West 110
Newcastle-under-Lyme 46
Newcastleton 74
Newhaven, Edinburgh 90
Newhaven, Sussex 26
Newick 26
Newington, Kent 28
Newington, Edinburgh 90
Newington, South London 34
Newlands 92
Newlyn 14
Newmarket 40
Newmarket, Munster 110

Newmarket-on-Fergus 110
Newport, Isle of Wight 22, 24
Newport (Casnewydd) 12, 18, 80, 82
Newport, Essex 36, 40
Newport-on-Tay 96
Newquay 14
Newry 110, 112
Newton 98
Newton Abbot 16, 18
Newton Ferrers 14, 16
Newton Longville 39
Newton Poppleford 16, 18
Newton St Cyres 16, 18
Newton-le-Willows 70
Newtown, Birmingham 50
Newtown, Wales 80
Newtownabbey 86, 110, 112
Newtownards 110, 112
Newtownbreda 114
Newtownbutler 110, 112
Newtownstewart 110, 112
Newtyle 96
Nidd, R. 56
Niddrie 88, 90
Niddry Burn 88
Niderdale 56
Ninfield 26, 28
Nisbet 74
Nith, R. 86
Nitshill 92
Nore 110
Normanton 58
North Baddesley 22
North Ballachulish 100
North Bull Island 116
North Cave 64
North Channel 12, 98, 112
North Chenton 18
North Dorset Downs 18
North Downs 22, 28
North Elmham 40
North Ferriby 54, 64
North Foreland 28
North Gyle 90
North Hykeham 54
North Kessock 104
North Leigh 39
North Molton 16, 18
North Queensferry 88
North Rnaldsay 106
North Roe 108
North Ronaldsay Firth 106
North Shields 74, 76
North Somercotes 54
North Sunderland 74
North Thoresby 54
North Tidworth 18, 22
North Tyne, R. 74
North Uist (Uibhist a Tuath) 86
North Walsham 40
North Weald 36
North York Moors 63
North York Moors National Park 56, 63
Northallerton 56
Northam, Devon 16
Northam, Northumberland 74
Northampton 12, 46
Northern Ireland 12, 86, 112
Northfleet 32
Northleach 39
Northumberland National Park 74
Northwich 46
Northwood 22, 24
Norton, East Anglia 40
Norton, Yorks. 56
Norton-Fitzwarren 16, 18
Norwich 12, 40, 42
Norwick 108
Notting Hill 34
Nottingham 12, 46
Noup Head 106
Nowen Hill 118
Nuneaton 46, 49
Nuthurst 26
Nyadd 94

O
Oakbank 88
Oakenshaw 58
Oakham 46
Oakley, Berks 22
Oakley, Bucks 39
Oakley, Scotland 88
Oatlands 92
Oban 100
Ockle 100
Oddsta 108
Odiham 22
Offerton 68
Ogmore 18, 82
Ogmore Vale 18, 82
Okehampton 14, 16
Old Basing 22
Old Colwyn 84
Old Felixstowe 36, 40
Old Head of Kinsale 110
Old Leake 64, 54
Old Town, Cumbria 72
Old Town, Edinburgh 90
Oldbury 46, 49
Oldhall 92
Oldham 52, 56, 66, 68
Oldland 18, 20
Ollaberry 108
Olveston 18
Omagh 110, 112
Onchan 78
Onich 100
Openshaw 68
Orchy, R. 100
Ordsall 68
Orford 40
Orford Ness 36, 40

Orkney Islands 12, 86, 106
Ormeau 114
Ormesby St Margaret 40, 42
Ormskirk 66, 70
Oronsay 98
Orpington 30, 32
Orrell 66, 70
Orrin, R. 104
Orrin Reservoir 104
Orton 72
Orwell, R. 36, 40
Oskaig 102
Ossett 58
Oswaldkirk 63
Oswaldtwistle 66
Oswestry 46, 80
Otford 28, 32
Otley, Suffolk 40
Otley, Yorks. 56
Otter, R. (nr Honiton) 16, 18
Otter Ferry 98
Otterburn 74
Otterswick 108
Ottery, R. 14, 16
Ottery St Mary 16, 18
Oughterard 110
Oulton 40, 42
Ouse, R. 26, 56
Out Skerries 108
Outer Hebrides 12, 86
Outwell 40, 44
Ouzel, R. 39
Over 20
Over Wallop 22
Overbister 106
Overton 22
Ox Mts (Slieve Gamph) 110
Oxford 12, 39
Oxgangs 90
Oxshott 30, 32
Oxted 30, 32
Oxton 74

P
Padbury 39
Paddington 34
Paddock Wood 28
Padiham 66
Padstow 14
Pagham 22, 26
Paignton 16
Painswick 39
Paisley 12, 86, 92
Palmerston 116
Pandy 82
Pangbourne 39
Pant, R. 36, 40
Papa Stour 108
Papa Stronsay 106
Papa Westray 106
Paps of Jura 98
Papworth Everard 40
Par 14
Parbold 66
Parkgate 60
Parkhead 92
Parknasilla 118
Parrett, R. 18
Parsons Green 34
Partick 92
Partington 66
Partney 54
Parton 72
Passage West 110
Patchway 18, 20
Patrick 78
Patrington 54, 64
Patterdale 72
Paulton 18
Paxton 74
Peacehaven 26
Peak District 60
Peak District National Park 46, 52
Peakeen Mountain 118
Peasedown 18
Peckham 34
Peebles 86
Peel 78
Pegwell Bay 28
Peinchorran 102
Pelsall 49
Pelynt 14, 16
Pembroke (Penfro) 80
Pembrokeshire Coast National Park 80
Pembury 26, 28
Pen-y-fai 18, 82
Pen-y-Ghent 56, 66
Penarth 18, 82
Pencoed 18, 82
Pendeen 14
Pendle Hill 66
Pendlebury 68
Peninver 98
Penistone 52, 56, 60
Penketh 70
Pennines 12
Pennyghael 100
Penrhyn Bay 84
Penrhyndeudraeth 84
Penrith 72
Penryn 14
Pensilva 14, 16
Pentir 84
Pentire Point 14
Pentland Firth 86, 106
Pentland Hills 88
Pentraeth 84
Penwortham 66
Penygadair 80
Penygroes 84
Penywaun 82
Penzance 14

Perranporth 14
Perranzabuloe 14
Perry 50
Perry Bar 50
Pershore 46
Perth 12, 86, 96
Perth, Wales 18
Peterborough 12, 40, 44
Peterlee 74
Petersfield 22, 26
Petworth 26
Pevensey 26
Pevensey Levels 26
Pewsey 22
Phoenix Park 116
Pickering 56, 63
Pictur 96
Piddle, R. 18
Piddletrenthide 18
Pierowall 106
Pillar 72
Pilling 66
Pilning 18
Pilton 90
Pimmill 98
Pimperne 18
Pinchbeck 40, 54
Pinhoe 16, 18
Pirbright 30
Pitminster 16, 18
Pitscottie 96
Pitt 22
Pladda 98
Plaistow 34
Plockton 102
Plymouth 12, 14, 16
Plympton 14, 16
Plymstock 14, 16
Plynlimon 80
Pocklington 56
Point of Ardnamurchan 86, 100
Point of Ayre 78
Point of Fethaland 108
Point of Knap 98
Point of Sleat 102
Polegate 26
Polesworth 49
Polloch 100
Pollock 92
Pollockshaws 92
Pollockshields 92
Polperro 14, 16
Polwarth 74
Pomeroy 112
Pondersbridge 40, 44
Pontardawe 82
Pontardulais 82
Pontefract 56, 58
Ponteland 74, 76
Pontsticill Reservoir 82
Pontyberem 82
Pontypool 80, 82
Pontypridd 18, 80, 82
Poole 18, 22
Poole Bay 18
Poolewe 102
Pooley Bridge 72
Poplar 34
Porlock 16, 18
Port Appin 100
Port Askaig 98
Port Bannatyne 98
Port Ellen 98
Port Erin 78
Port Eynon 82
Port Glasgow 98
Port Henderson 102
Port Isaac Bay 14
Port Láirge (Waterford) 12, 110
Port of Monteith 94
Port St Mary 78
Port Sunlight 70
Port Talbot 18, 80, 82
Portadown 110, 112
Portaferry 110, 112
Portarlington 110
Portchester 22, 24
Portencross 98
Portesham 18
Porth 82
Porthcawl 18, 80, 82
Porthleven 14
Porthmadog 80, 84
Portishead 18
Portland 20
Portland Harbour 18
Portlaoise 12, 110
Portmagee 118
Portnacroish 100
Portnahaven 98
Portnalong 102
Portobello 88, 90
Portreath 14
Portree 86, 102
Portrush 110, 112
Portsmouth 12, 22, 24
Portstewart 110, 112
Portumna 110
Possil Park 92
Potterne 18
Potters Bar 32, 39
Potton 40
Poulgorm Bridge 118
Poulton-le-Fylde 66
Powburn 74
Poynton 52, 56, 66
Prawle Point 16
Preesall 66
Prescot 70
Prestatyn 66
Presteigne 80
Prestolee 68
Preston, Dorset 18
Preston, East Riding 64
Preston, Lancs. 12, 66

Prestwich 68
Prestwick 98
Prestwood 39
Priesthill 92
Priestholm (Puffin Island) 84
Princes Risborough 39
Princetown 14, 16
Probus 14
Prudhoe 74
Puddletown 18
Pudsey 58
Puffin Island (Priestholm) 84
Pulborough 26
Puriton 16, 18
Purfleet 28, 32, 36
Purley 30, 32
Purley on Thames 22
Purple Mountain 118
Purton 18, 39
Putney 34
Pwllheli 80, 84
Pyle 18, 82

Q
Quantock Hills 16, 18
Quarries 100
Queen Charlton 20
Queenborough 28
Queensbury 58
Queensferry 70

R
Rackheath 40, 42
Rackwick 106
Radcliffe 68
Radlett 32, 39
Radley 116
Rainford 66, 70
Rainow 52
Rait 96
Ralston 92
Rame 14, 16
Rame Head 14, 16
Ramelton 104
Ramsbottom 56
Ramsbury 22
Ramsey 40, 44
Ramsey Bay 78
Ramsey Island 80
Ramsey, Isle of Man 78
Ramsey St Mary's 40, 44
Ramsgate 28
Rathfarnham 116
Rathgar 116
Rathillet 96
Rathlin Island 98, 110, 112
Rathluirc 110
Rathmines 116
Rathmore 118
Ratho 88
Rattray 96
Ravenfield 60
Ravenglass 72
Rawdon 58
Rawmarsh 60
Rawtenstall 66
Rayleigh 36
Rayne 36, 40
Rea, R. 50
Reading 22
Read's Island 64
Reanagowan 118
Reananeree 118
Red Wharf Bay 82
Redbourn 39
Redcar 56
Redcastle 104
Redcliff Bay 18
Redditch 46
Rede 74
Redford 96
Redhill 30
Redland 20
Redlynch 18, 22
Redpoint 102
Redruth 14
Reen 118
Reepham 40
Regaby 78
Regent's Park 34
Reigate 30
Renfrew 92
Rennington 74
Resolven 82
Restalrig 90
Retford 56
Reydon 40
Rhondda 18, 82
Rhoose 18, 82
Rhôs-on-Sea 84
Rhossili 82
Rhu 94, 98
Rhuthun (Ruthin) 80
Rhyl 80, 84
Rhymney 82
Ribble, R. 56, 66
Ribblesdale 56, 66
Riccal, R. 63
Riccarton Hills 88
Richmond 12
Richmond, Yorks. 56
Rickinghall 40
Rickmansworth 32, 39
Riddrie 92
Ridgacre 50
Riding Mill 74
Ringland 40
Ringmer 26
Ringwood 18, 22
Rinns of Islay 98
Rinns Point 98
Ripley 56
Ripon 56
Ripple 39
Ripple 39

Ripponden 56
Risca 18, 82
Roadford Reservoir 14, 16
Roan Fell 74
Roaringwater Bay 110
Roath 18, 82
Roberton 74
Robin Hood's Bay 63
Rochdale 56, 66
Roche 14
Rochester, Kent 28
Rochester, Northumberland 74
Rochford 36
Rockingham Forest 46
Rockwell Green 16, 18
Rodney Stoke 18
Roe, R. 112
Rogate 22, 26
Rogerstone 18, 82
Rois-Bheinn 100
Roker 74
Rollesby 40, 42
Roman, R. 36, 40
Romanby 56
Rombalds Moor 58
Romford 32, 36
Romney Marsh 28
Romsey 22
Romsley 49
Rona 102
Ronas Hill 108
Roos 64
Roscommon 110
Roscrea 110
Rose Ness 106
Roseberry Topping 63
Rosedale Abbey 63
Rosemarkie 104
Roshven 100
Roskhill 102
Ross of Mull 100
Ross-on-Wye 80
Rossan Point 110
Rosses Bay 112
Rosslare 110
Rosslare Harbour 110
Rostrevor 112
Rosyth 88
Rothbury 74
Rothbury Forest 74
Rother, R. 22, 26
Rother (Yorks), R. 60
Rotherfield 26, 28
Rotherham 56, 60
Rotherhithe 34
Rothesay 98
Rothiesholm 106
Rothwell 58
Rottingdean 26
Rough Point 118
Roughton 40
Roughty, R. 118
Round Hill 63
Roundhay 58
Roundway 18
Rousay 86, 106
Rowden 18
Rowlands Gill 76
Roxton 40
Royal Canal 110, 116
Royal Leamington Spa 46
Royal Tunbridge Wells 26, 28
Roydon 40
Royston 36, 39, 40
Royston, Glasgow 92
Royton 52
Rubh' a'Geodha 98
Rubh' a'Mhuil 98
Rubha Hunish 102
Rubha na Traille 98
Rubha nan Leacan 98
Ruchaize 92
Rudgwick 26, 30
Rufford 66
Rugby 46
Rugeley 46
Rum 86, 102
Rumney 18, 82
Runcorn 66, 70, 80
Runwell 36
Rushall 49
Rushden 46
Rushmere St Andrew 40
Rusholme 68
Ruskington 54
Rustington 26
Rutherglen 92
Ruthin (Rhuthun) 80
Rutland Water 46
Ryde 22, 24
Rye 26, 28
Rye Bay 26, 28
Rye, R. 56, 63

S
Sacriston 74
Saddell 98
Saffron Walden 36, 40
Saham Toney 40
St Agnes 14
St Albans 39
St Alban's Head 18
St Andrews 96
St Anne's Park 116
St Athan 18, 82
St Austell 14
St Austell Bay 14
St Bees 72
St Bees Head 72
St Bride's Bay 80
St Brides Major 18, 82
St Buryan 14
St Catherine's Point 24

St Clears 80
St Columb Major 14
St David's Head 80
St David's (Tyddewi) 80
St Day 14
St Dennis 14
St Endellion 14
St Enodet 14
St Erth 14
St Finan's Bay 118
St Gennys 14
St George's Channel 12
St Germans 14, 16
St Govan's Head 80
St Helens 66, 70
St Ive 14, 16
St Ives 40
St Ives Bay 14
St John Radstock 18
St John's Chapel 74
St John's Wood 34
St Just 14
St Just in Roseland 14
St Keverne 14
St Leonards 18, 22
St Magnus Bay 108
St Margaret's at Cliffe 28
St Margaret's Hope 106
St Mary Bourne 22
St Mary in the Marsh 28
St Mary's 106
St Mary's Bay 28
St Mawes 14
St Merryn 14
St Michael's Mount 14
St Neots 40
St Ninian's Isle 108
St Osyth 36, 40
St Peter's 28
St Stephen 14
St Teath 14
Saintfield 110
Salcombe 16
Sale 56, 66, 68
Salehurst 26, 28
Salen 100
Sales Point 36
Salford 56, 66, 68
Salford Quays 68
Salfords 30
Salhouse 40, 42
Saliahig 118
Saline 88
Salisbury 18, 22
Salisbury Plain 18
Saltash 14, 16
Saltburn-by-the-Sea 56, 63
Saltcoats 98
Saltdean 26
Saltfords 30
Salter Islands 110
Saltford 18, 20
Saltley 50
Sanaigmore 98
Sanda Island 98
Sanday 86, 106
Sanday Sound 106
Sandbach 46
Sandgarth 106
Sandhurst 22, 30
Sandness 108
Sandown 24
Sandplace 14, 16
Sandridge 39, 40
Sandsend 63
Sandwell 50
Sandwich 28
Sandwick 108
Sandy 40
Sandygate 78
Sandymount 116
Santry 116
Sarre 28
Saughall 70
Sawbridgeworth 36, 40
Sawel Mountain 112
Sawston 40
Sawtry 40
Saxa Vord 108
Saxilby 54
Saxmundham 40
Saxthorpe 40
Scafell Pike 12, 72
Scalasaig 98
Scalby 56, 63
Scalloway 108
Scalp Mountain 112
Scalpay 102
Scampton 54
Scapa 106
Scapa Flow 106
Scarba 98
Scarborough 56, 63
Scarcroft 58
Scariff Island 110, 118
Scarinish 100
Scarisbrick 66
Scartaglen 118
Scartho 64
Scholes 58
Schull 110
Sconser 102
Scote 40
Scotstoun 92
Scotter 54, 56
Scotton 56
Scottow 40, 42
Scousburgh 108
Scremerston 74
Scunthorpe 54, 56, 64
Sea of the Hebrides 102
Seacombe 70
Seaford 26
Seaforth 70
Seaham 74, 76

Seahouses 74
Seamer 63
Seamill 98
Seascale 72
Seaton, Cumbria 72
Seaton Delaval 74, 76
Seaton, Devon 16, 18
Seaton Sluice 74, 76
Seaview 22, 24
Sedbergh 72
Sedgley 49
Seend 18
Seil 100
Selby 56
Selfindge 28
Selkirk 74
Sellafield 72
Sellafirth 108
Selsey 22, 26
Selsey Bill 22, 26
Sennen 14
Setter 108
Settle 56, 66
Seven, R. 63
Seven Sisters 82
Sevenoaks 28, 32
Severn, R. 12, 39, 46, 80
Severn Beach 18
Sgarbh Breac 98
Sgorr Ruadh 102
Sgurr a'Choire Ghlais 104
Sgurr Alasdair 102
Sgurr a'Mhuilinn 104
Sgurr Dhomhnuill 100
Sgurr Fhuaran 102
Sgurr na Ciche 102
Shacklewell 34
Shadowlands 92
Shaftesbury 18
Shalfleet 22, 24
Shalford 30
Shanacashel 118
Shandon 94
Shankill 114
Shanklin 24
Shannon, R. 110, 112
Shannon Airport 110
Shap 72
Shapinsay 106
Shapinsay Sound 106
Sharron, R. 12
Shaw 66
Sheep Haven 110
Sheering 36, 40
Sheerness 28
Sheffield 46, 52, 56
Shefford 39, 40
Shehy Mts. 118
Shenstone 49
Shepperton 30, 32
Shepton Mallet 18
Sherborne 18
Sherborne St John 22
Sherburn 74
Sherburn in Elmet 56
Shercock 110
Shere 30
Shering 40
Sherston 18, 39
Sherwood Forest 46
Shetland Islands 12, 86, 108
Shettleston 92
Shiddaw 72
Shiel Bridge 102
Shieldaig 102
Shielhall 92
Shilbottle 74
Shillelagh 110
Shinfield 22
Shining Tor 46
Shiplake 22
Shipley 56, 58
Shipston on Stour 39
Shipton-under-Wychwood 39
Shira, R. 100
Shirehampton 20
Shirenewton 18
Shoeburyness 36
Shoreditch 34
Shoreham 28, 32
Shoreham-by-Sea 26
Short Heath 50
Shotley Gate 36, 40
Shotton 70
Shrewsbury 12, 46, 80
Shrewton 18, 22
Sible Hedingham 36, 40
Sibsey 40, 54
Sidbury 16, 18
Sidford 16, 18
Sidlaw Hills 86, 96
Sidley 26
Sidmouth 16, 18
Sighthill 90
Silecroft 72
Silksworth 76
Sillogue Park 116
Silver End 36, 40
Silverdale 66, 72
Silverknowles 90
Silverton 16, 18
Simonsbath 16, 18
Sion Mills 112
Siston 20
Sittingbourne 28
Skaill 106
Skara Brae 106
Skaw 108
Skeld 108
Skelda Ness 108
Skellig Rocks 118
Skelmersdale 66

Skelmorlie 98
Skelton 63
Skelwick 106
Skerries 110
Skibbereen 12, 110
Skipness 98
Skipton 56
Skomer Island 80
Skye 12, 86, 102
Slarney, R. 110
Slea, R. 54
Slea Head 110, 118
Sleaford 46, 54
Sleat 102
Sleights 56, 63
Slievanea 118
Slieve Anierin 112
Slieve Bloom Mts 110
Slieve Car 110
Slieve Donard 110
Slieve Gamph (Ox Mts) 110
Slieve League 112
Slieve Mish Mts 110, 118
Sligachan 102
Sligo 12, 110
Sligo Bay 112
Sligo (Sligeach) 110, 112
Slinfold 26, 30
Slioch 102
Slough 32
Slyne Head 110
Smailholm 74
Small Heath 50
Small Isles 98
Smeeth 28
Smerwick 118
Smerwick Harbour 118
Smethwick 49, 50
Snaefell 78
Snaith 56
Snaiton 63
Snave Bridge 118
Sneem 110, 118
Snettisham 40, 54
Snodland 28
Snowdon 12, 80, 84
Snowdonia National Park 80, 84
Soa Island 100
Soay 102
Soham 40, 44
Solihull 46, 49
Solway Firth 12, 86
Somersham 40, 44
Somerton 18
Sompting 26
Sonning Common 22
Sorisdale 100
Sorrento Point 116
Sound of Arisaig 100
Sound of Bute 98
Sound of Canna 102
Sound of Gigha 98
Sound of Iona 100
Sound of Islay 98
Sound of Jura 86, 98
Sound of Mull 86, 100
Sound of Raasay 102
Sound of Sleat 86, 102
Soundwell 20
South Anston 60
South Benfleet 36
South Cave 64
South Cerney 18, 39
South Chard 16, 18
South Dorset Downs 18
South Downs 26
South Gyle 90
South Harting 22, 26
South Hetton 74
South Hylton 76
South Kelsey 54
South Lopham 40
South Molton 16, 18
South Nesting Bay 108
South Ockendon 32, 36
South Oxhey 32, 39
South Petherton 18
South Queensferry 88
South Ronaldsay 106
South Shields 74, 76, 86
South Skirlaugh 56
South Tyne, R. 74
South Uist (Uibhist a'Deas) 86
South Walls 106
South Woodham-Ferrers 36
South Wootton 40
South Yardley 50
Southampton 12, 22
Southampton Water 22, 24
Southborough 26, 28
Southbourne 22
Southdean 74
Southend, Kintyre 98
Southend-on-Sea 36
Southern Uplands 12, 86
Southery 40, 44
Southfields 34
Southgate 32, 39
Southminster 36
Southowram 58
Southport 66
Southwark 34
Southwater 26
Southwick, Tyne and Wear 76
Southwick, Wiltshire 18
Southwold 40
Sowerby 63
Sowerby Bridge 56, 58
Spa 118
Spalding 40
Span Head 16, 18
Spanish Point 110
Sparkbrook 50
Sparkhill 50

Speen 22
Speke 70
Spennymoor 74
Sperrin Mts 110
Spey, R. 12, 104
Spilsby 54
Spixworth 40, 42
Springboig 92
Springburn 92
Springwell 76
Sproatley 64
Sprowston 40, 42
Sproxton 63
Spurn Head 54, 56, 64
Squires Hill 114
Stadhampton 39
Staffa 100
Staffin 102
Staffin Bay 102
Stafford 46
Staines 30, 32
Staintondale 63
Stalbridge 18
Stalham 40, 42
Stalybridge 52
Stamford 46
Stamford Bridge 56
Stamfordham 74
Stamperland 92
Standish 66
Standon 36, 40
Stanford le Hope 36
Stanhoe 40
Stanhope 74
Stanley 74, 76
Stanley, Scotland 96
Stannington, Yorks. 60
Stannington, Northumberland 74
Stanstead Airport 36, 40
Stansted Mountfitchet 36, 40
Stanton 40
Stanway 36, 40
Stanwix 74
Staplehurst 28
Stapleton 20
Starcross 16, 18
Start Bay 16
Start Point 16
Staveley 46
Staxton 63
Steep Holm, Is. 18, 82
Steeping, R. 54
Steeple Claydon 39
Stenhouse 90
Stenness 108
Steomabhagh (Stornoway) 12, 86
Stepaside 116
Stevenage 39, 40
Stevenston 98
Steyning 26
Stibb Cross 16
Stichill 74
Stickney 54
Stillorgan 116
Stilton 40
Stirling 12, 86, 94
Stithians 14
Stock 36
Stockbridge 22
Stockport 56, 66, 68
Stocks Reservoir 66
Stocksbridge 52, 56, 60
Stocksfield 74
Stockton Heath 70
Stockton-on-Tees 56, 63
Stockwood 20
Stogursey 16, 18
Stoke Ash 40
Stoke Gifford 20
Stoke Holy Cross 40, 42
Stoke Mandeville 39
Stoke Newington 34
Stoke Poges 32
Stoke St Mary 16, 18
Stoke sub Hamdon 18
Stoke-by-Nayland 36, 40
Stoke-on-Trent 46
Stokenchurch 39
Stokenham 16
Stokesley 56, 63
Stone 18
Stonehaven 86
Stonehenge 18, 22
Stony Stratford 39
Stornoway (Steomabhagh) 12, 86
Storrington 26
Stort, R. 36, 40
Stotfold 39, 40
Stour, R. 18, 46
Stour (Kent), R. 28
Stour, R. 36, 40
Stourbridge 46, 49
Stourport-on-Severn 46
Stow 74
Stow-on-the-Wold 39
Stowmarket 40
Strabane 110, 112
Stradbally 118
Stradbroke 40
Stradishall 40
Stradsett 40, 44
Strait of Dover 12
Strait of Dover 28
Strangeways 68
Strangford 112
Strangford Lough 110, 112
Stranocum 112
Stranraer 86
Stratfield Mortimer 22
Stratford 34
Stratford-upon-Avon 46
Strath Dearn, R. 104
Strathblane 94
Strathconon 104

Strathglass, R. 104
Strathmore 96
Strathpeffer 104
Strathspey, R. 86
Strathyre 94
Stratton 14, 16
Streatley 22
Street 18
Stretford 66, 68
Stretham 40, 44
Stromeferry 102
Stromemore 102
Stromness 106
Stronachlachar 94
Strone 98
Stronsay 106
Stronsay Firth 106
Strontian 100
Stroud 39
Strumble Head 80
Stubb Cross 14
Stubbington 22, 24
Stuckgowan 94
Stuckindroin 94
Studham 39
Studland 18
Sturminster Newton 18
Sturry 28
Suck, R. 110
Sudbury 36, 40
Sugarloaf Mountain 118
Suir, R. 110
Sullington 26
Sullom Voe 108
Sully 18, 82
Sumburgh 108
Sumburgh Head 12, 86, 108
Sunbury 30, 32
Sunderland 74, 76, 86
Sunninghill 30
Surfleet 40, 54
Sutterton 40, 54
Sutton in Ashfield 46
Sutton Bridge 40
Sutton, Cambs. 40, 44
Sutton Coldfield 46, 49
Sutton Courtenay 39
Sutton, Dublin 116
Sutton Valence 28
Swadlincote 46
Swaffham 40
Swale, R. 56
Swanage 18
Swanley 28, 32
Swanlinbar 110
Swansea (Abertawe) 12, 80, 82
Swansea Bay 80, 82
Swarton Morley 40
Sway 22, 24
Swindon 18, 22, 39
Swineshead 40, 54
Swinton, Greater Manchester 66
Swinton, Northumberland 74
Swinton, Yorks. 60
Swona 106
Swords 110
Sybil Point 118
Sydenham 114
Symbister 108

T
Tadcastle 56
Tadley 22
Taffs Well 18, 82
Tahilla 118
Tain 86
Takeley 36, 40
Talisket 102
Talladale 102
Tallaght 116
Tamar, R. 14, 16
Tame, R. 50, 68
Tamworth 46, 49
Tarbert 98
Tarbert, Rep. of Ireland 110
Tarbet 94
Tarvin 70
Tattershall 54
Taunton 16, 18
Taverham 40, 42
Tavistock 14, 16
Tavy, R. 14, 16
Taw 16
Taw, R. 16
Tawe, R. 82
Tay, R. 86, 96
Tayinloan 98
Taynuilt 100
Tayport 96
Tayvallich 98
Teangue 102
Tebay 72
Teeranearagh 118
Tees, R. 12, 56, 72
Teesside Airport 56
Teifi, R. 80
Teign, R. 16, 18
Teignmouth 16, 18
Teith, R. 94
Telford 12, 46, 80
Teme, R. 46, 80
Temple Ewell 28
Temple Sowerby 72
Templemore 110
Templenoe 118
Tenby 80
Tenterden 26, 28
Tentsmuir Forest 96
Terenure 116
Tern, R. 46, 80
Terrington Marsh 40, 54
Terrington St Clement 40
Test, R. 22
Tetbury 18, 39

Tetford 54
Tetney 54, 64
Teviot, R. 74
Teviotdale 74
Teviothead 74
Tewkesbury 39, 46
Texa 98
Teynham 28
Thame 39
Thame, R. 39
Thames, R. 12, 22, 28, 32, 34, 36, 39
Thatcham 22
Thaxted 36, 40
The Broads 40, 42
The Calf 72
The Cheviot 74
The Faither 108
The Fens 40
The Minch 12, 86, 102
The Mullet 110
The Mumbles 82
The Naze 36
The Needles 24
The North Sound 106
The Old Man of Coniston 72
The Paps 118
The Pocket 118
The Rosses 112
The Seven Hogs 118
The Solent 22, 24
The Sound 14, 16
The Starr 102
The Stocks 26, 28
The Swale 28
The Trossachs 94
The Wash 40
The Weald 26
Thet, R. 40
Thetford 40
Thirlmere 72
Thirsk 56, 63
Thomastown 110
Thornaby-on-Tees 63
Thornbury 18
Thorne 56
Thorner 58
Thorney 40, 44
Thorngumbald 64
Thornhill 94
Thornley 74
Thornliebank 92
Thornton 66, 70
Thornton Dale 63
Thorpe Market 40
Thorpe St Andrew 40, 42
Thorpe-le-Soken 36, 40
Thorpeness 40
Threlkeld 72
Thropton 74
Thrybergh 60
Thundersley 36
Thurcroft 60
Thurgoland 60
Thurles 110
Thurso, R. 86
Thurstaston 70
Thurston 40
Thurton 40, 42
Ticehurst 26, 28
Tickhill 60
Tideswell 52
Tiduff 118
Tighnabruaich 98
Tilbury 28, 36
Tildenham 18
Tilehurst 22
Till, R. 74
Timperley 68
Tingewick 39
Tingwall 106, 108
Tinsley 60
Tintagel 14
Tipperary 110
Tiptree 36, 40
Tiree 86, 100
Tisbury 18
Tiverton 16, 18
Toab 108
Tobermory 100
Toddington, Beds. 39
Toddington, Glos. 39
Todhills 96
Toft 108
Togston 74
Tolka River 116
Tollesbury 36
Tolleshunt D'Arcy 36, 40
Tomatin 104
Tonbridge 28
Tone, R. 16, 18
Tonna 18, 82
Tonyrefail 18, 82
Topsham 16, 18
Tor Bay 16
Tormore 98
Torne, R. 56
Torpoint 14, 16
Torquay 12, 16
Torridge, R. 14, 16
Torridon 102
Torrin 102
Torside Reservoir 52
Torver 72
Tory Island 110, 112
Tory Sound 110, 112
Toscaig 102
Totland 22, 24
Totnes 16
Totton 22
Tove, R. 46
Tow Law 74
Towcester 46
Townhill 88
Towyn 84

Trá Li (Tralee) 118
Trachur 98
Traford Park 68
Tralee 118
Tralee Bay 118
Tralee (Trá Li) 12, 110, 118
Tramore 110
Trawsfynydd 84
Tredegar 82
Trefaldwyn (Montgomery) 80
Trefriw 84
Trefynwy (Monmouth) 80
Tregony 14
Trelissick 14
Tremadog 84
Tremadog Bay 84
Trenance 14
Trent, R. 12, 18, 46, 54, 56
Treorchy 18, 82
Treshnish Isles 100
Tretower 82
Trevose Head 14
Triangle 58
Trillick 112
Trim 110
Trimdon 72
Trimley St Mary 36, 40
Trimsbury 18
Tring 39
Troney, R. 16, 18
Troon 98
Trostan 110
Trotternish 102
Troutbeck 72
Troutbeck Bridge 72
Trowbridge 18
Trull 16, 18
Trumpington 40
Truro 14
Truskmore 110
Tuam 110
Tullamore (Tulach Mhór) 110
Tulleycarnet 114
Tullow 110
Tunstall 40
Turf Lodge 114
Turnberry 98
Turners Hill 26, 30
Tutshill 18
Twatt 106
Tweed, R. 12, 74, 86
Tweedmouth 74
Twyford 22
Twyning 39
Tybarn 98
Tyddewi (St David's) 80
Tymon Park 116
Tyne, R. 74, 76
Tyne and Wear 74, 76
Tynemouth 74, 76
Tythegston 18, 82
Tywardreath 14
Tywi, R. 80

U
Uamh Bheag 94
Uckfield 26
Uffculme 16, 18
Ugborough 16
Uibhist a'Deas (South Uist) 86
Uibhist a Tuath (North Uist) 86
Ulceby 54, 64
Ulgham 74
Ullapool 86
Ullswater 72
Ulpha 72
Ulsta 108
Ulva 100
Ulverston 66, 72
Umberleigh 16
Undy 18
Unst 12, 86, 108
Unyeasound 108
Upavon 18, 22
Uplyme 16, 18
Upper Breakish 102
Upper Clatford 22
Upper Heyford 39
Upper Lough Erne 110, 112
Upton 70
Urafirth 108
Ure, R. 56
Urmston 68
Ushaw Moor 74
Usk, R. 18, 80, 82
Uxbridge 32, 39
Uyea 108

V
Vaila 108
Vale of Ely 82
Vale of Evesham 46
Vale of Glamorgan 18
Vale of Gloucester 39
Vale of Kent 28
Vale of Pewsey 18, 22
Vale of Pickering 56, 63
Vale of York 56
Valencia Island 110, 118
Valleyfield 88
Vaternish Point 102
Ventnor 24
Ventry 118
Verwood 18, 22
Vickerstown 72
Victoria Park 34
Vidlin 108
Virginia Water 30
Voe 108

W
Waddesdon 39
Waddington 54
Wadebridge 14
Wadhurst 26
Wadsley Bridge 60

Wadworth 60
Wainfleet All Saints 54
Wainhouse Corner 14, 16
Wakefield 56, 58
Walberswick 40
Walderslade 28
Waldon, R. 14, 16
Wallasey 66, 70
Wallbottle 76
Wallingford 39
Walls 108
Wallsend 74, 76
Walmer 28
Walsall 46, 49
Walsoken 40, 44
Waltham 54, 64
Waltham Abbey 32
Waltham on the Wolds 54
Walton 70
Walton-on-Thames 30, 32
Walton-on-The-Naze 36, 40
Walworth 34
Wandsworth 30, 32, 34
Wantage 39
Warboys 40, 44
Warcop 72
Ward of Bressay 108
Ward Hill 106
Ward's Stone 66
Ware 36, 39, 40
Wareham 18
Wargrave 22
Wark 74
Warkworth 74
Warley 50
Warlingham 30, 32
Warminster 18
Warmley 20
Warmley, West Midlands 50
Warmsworth 60
Warnham 26, 30
Warrenpoint 110, 112
Warrington 66, 70
Warton 66, 72
Warwick 46
Warwick Bridge 74
Warburn 76
Wasbister 106
Washington 74, 76
Washwood Heath 50
Wass 63
Wast Water 72
Watchet 16, 18
Watchgate 72
Water of Leith 88, 90
Water Orton 49
Waterbeach 40
Waterford Harbour 110
Waterford (Port Láirge) 12, 110
Watergate Bay 14
Waterlooville 22
Waterville 110, 118
Watford 32, 39
Wath-upon-Dearne 60
Watlington 39
Watton 40
Watton-at-Stone 40
Waveney, R. 40, 42
Wear, R. 74, 76, 86
Weaver, R. 70
Weaverham 70
Wedland, R. 46
Wedmore 18
Wednesbury 49
Weisdale 108
Welland, R. 40, 54
Wellbank 96
Wellingborough 46
Wellington 16, 18
Wells 18
Wells-next-the-Sea 40
Wellwood 88
Welney 40, 44
Welshpool (Y Trallwng) 46, 80
Welton 54, 56
Welwick 64
Welwyn 39, 40
Welwyn Garden City 39, 40
Wem 46
Wembdon 16, 18
Wembley 32
Wemyss Bay 98
Wendens Ambo 36, 40
Wendover 39
Wendron 14
Wenlock Edge 46
Wenning, R. 66, 72
Wensleydale 56
Wensum, R. 40
Wereham 40, 44
West Bergholt 36, 40
West Bridgford 46
West Brompton 34
West Bromwich 46, 49, 50
West Coker 18
West Derby 70
West Fen, Cambs. 40, 44
West Fen, Lincs. 40, 54
West Grinstead 26
West Ham 34
West Harptree 18
West Kilbride 98
West Kirkby 66, 70
West Knapton 63
West Lavington 18
West Loch Tarbert 98
West Looe 14, 16
West Lulworth 18
West Malling 28
West Meon 22
West Mersea 36, 40
West Monkton 16, 18
West Moors 18, 22
West Rainton 74
West Somerton 40, 42
West Town 22

West Town, Tory Island 110
West Wellow 22
West Wemyss 88
West Wycombe 39
West Yell 108
Westbury 18
Westbury Park 20
Westbury-on-Trym 20
Westcott 30
Westergate 22, 26
Westerham 30, 32
Westfield 26, 28
Westgate 74
Westing 108
Westleton 40
Westminster 34
Westness 106
Weston 18
Weston-super-Mare 18, 80, 82
Westonzoyland 18
Westport 12, 110
Westray 106
Westray Firth 106
Westruther 74
Westward Ho! 16
Wetheral 74
Wetherby 56
Wexford 12, 110
Wexford Harbour 110
Weybridge 30, 32
Weymouth 18
Whaley Bridge 52
Whalley Range 68
Whalsay 108
Whalton 74
Whaplode 40, 54
Wharfe, R. 56, 66
Wharfedale 56
Wheddon Cross 16, 18
Whernside 56, 66, 72
Wherwell 22
Whickham 74, 76
Whiddon Down 16, 18
Whimple 16, 18
Whiston 60
Whitburn 76
Whitby 56, 63, 70
Whitchurch, Bucks. 39
Whitchurch, Hants. 22
Whitchurch, N.Somerset 18, 20
Whitchurch, Shropshire 80
Whitchurch, Wales 82
White Car Water 92
Whitechapel 34
Whitecraig 88
Whitefield 68
Whitehall 20
Whitehall, Stronsay 106
Whitehaven 72
Whitehead 112
Whitehill 22, 26
Whiteinch 92
Whitewell 114
Whitfield 28
Whitford 70
Whiting Bay 98
Whitkirk 58
Whitley Bay 74, 76
Whitsand Bay 14, 16
Whitstable 28
Whittingham 74
Whittlesey 40, 44
Whitworth 66
Wibsey 58
Wick, Scotland 86
Wick, Sussex 26
Wick, Wales 18, 82
Wickersley 60
Wickford 36
Wickham 22
Wickham Market 40
Wicklow 12, 110
Wicklow Head 110
Wicklow Mts 12, 110
Wicklow Mts National Park 110
Wickwar 18
Wide Firth 106
Widecombe in the Moor 16, 18
Widford 36, 40
Widnes 46, 66, 70, 80
Wigan 66, 70
Wigston 46
Wigtown 86
Willand 16, 18
Willaston 70
Willesden 34
Willingdon 26
Willingham 40
Willington 74, 76
Williton 16, 18
Willoughby 54
Wilmslow 46, 66
Wilsden 58
Wilton 18, 22
Wimbleball Lake 16, 18
Wimblington 40, 44
Wimborne Minster 18, 22
Wincanton 18
Winchburgh 88
Winchelsea 26, 28
Winchester 12, 22
Wincobank 60
Windermere 72
Windlestraw Law 74
Windmill Hill 20
Windrush, R. 39
Windsor 30
Windsor, Belfast 114
Windy Gyle 74
Winford 18
Wing 39
Wingate 74
Wingham 28
Winkfield 22, 30
Winkleigh 16

Winlaton 76
Winnersh 22
Winscombe 18
Winsford 46, 70
Winsley 18
Winslow 39
Winterbourne 18, 20
Winterbourne Abbas 18
Winterton 54, 64
Wirral 46, 66, 70
Wisbech 40, 44
Witham 36, 40
Witham, R. 40, 54
Witheridge 16, 18
Withernsea 56, 64
Withington 68
Withywood 20
Witley 26, 30
Witney 39
Witton 50
Witton Gilbert 74
Wiveliscombe 16, 18
Wivenhoe 36, 40
Woburn 39
Woburn Sands 39
Woking 30, 32
Wokingham 22, 30
Wolf Hill 114
Wolsingham 74
Wolverhampton 46, 49
Wolverton 39
Wombourne 49
Wombwell 60
Wonston 22
Wooburn 39
Woodbridge 36, 40
Woodcote 22
Woodhall Spa 54
Woodhouse 60
Woodingdean 26
Woodley 22
Woodmancote 39
Woodplumpton 66
Woodstock 39
Woodton 40, 42
Woodvale 114
Wool 18
Woolacombe 16
Wooler 74
Woolwich 32
Wootton Bassett 18, 22
Worcester 12, 46
Workington 72
Worksop 46, 56, 60
Wormit 96
Worms Head 80
Worplesdon 30
Worsbrough 60
Worsley 68
Worth 26, 30
Worthing 26
Wotton-under-Edge 18, 39
Woughton on the Green 39
Wragby 54
Wrangle 40, 54
Wreake, R. 46
Wrelton 63
Wrenthorpe 58
Wrexham (Wrecsam) 46, 80
Wrington 18
Writtle 36
Wroughton 18, 22
Wyberton 40, 54
Wye 28
Wye, R. 18, 46, 80
Wyke 58
Wyle, R. 18, 22
Wymondham 40
Wyre 106
Wyre, R. 66
Wythall 49

Y
Y Fenni (Abergavenny) 80, 82
Y Fflint (Flint) 70, 80
Y Trallwng (Welshpool) 46, 80
Yam 63
Yapton 26
Yardley 50
Yare, R. 40, 42
Yarm 56
Yarmouth 22, 24
Yarnton 39
Yate 18
Yateley 22
Yatton 18
Yaxley 40
Yeadon 58
Yealmpton 14, 16
Yell 86, 108
Yell Sound 108
Yeo, R. 16, 18
Yeovil 18
Yeovilton 18
Yes Tor 14, 16
Yesnaby 106
Ynsddu 18
Ynys Mon (Anglesey) 12, 80, 84
Ynysddu 82
York 12
Yorker 92
Yorkshire Dales National Park 56, 66
Yorkshire Wolds 56
Youghal 110
Yoxford 40
Ystalyfera 82
Ystradgynlais 82

Z
Zennor 14